The Internet has taken over our lives. Computers were more a novelty twenty years ago but have grown into a necessity. Every facet of our lives has been affected.

Life and Death on the Internet is the first book that really tackles the issues of Internet safety head-on. This book shows you where the worst pornography and other Internet indecencies are. Then, in a simple step-by-step process you are shown how to prevent your children access to these areas. You are also shown how to detect if your children have ever visited these illicit Newsgroups or Websites.

Life and Death on the Internet is not only a must for parents, businesses need this book, too. With liability risks around every corner in the business world you must keep employees from infecting your computer system with illegal material. Pornography acquired or brought to work could result in a sexual harassment lawsuit. *Life and Death on the Internet* even shows you how to clean your system if it is infected with pornography, even if the indecent files are hidden.

Protect your children, your business, yourself, and your family. We live in a brave new world. You can live with it, or die by it. The choice is yours.

Life and Death on the Internet

How to Protect Your Family on the World Wide Web

Supple Publishing

1535 Plank Road
Menasha, WI 54952

Published by: Supple Publishing
1535 Plank Road
Menasha, WI 54952

Printed in the United States by the George Banta Corporation

Library of Congress Catalog Card Number: 98-96530

ISBN: 0-9666442-0-4

Cover by: Graphic Composition, Inc.

This publication is designed to provide accurate and authoritative information in regard to the subject matter covered. It is sold with the understanding that neither author nor the publisher is engaged in rendering legal, accounting, or other professional service. If any legal advice or other assistance is required, the services of a competent professional person should be sought.

--From the Declaration of Principles jointly adopted by a Committee of the American Bar Association and a Committee of Publishers.

It is the advice of the author that professional legal advice should be sought from a competent legal professional before entering the Internet.

To my family:

My wife, Sue
My daughter, Heather
My parents

Their love has granted me the time to write this book.

My love required that I write it.

Apology

There are some that will say this book is too long or too technical. Some will say this book is not long enough or technical enough. To all who make such claims I accept full responsibility.

I agree that this book is too long and too short. I made every effort to be as complete as possible without being redundant.

The Internet can easily get technical when discussed. Every effort was made to keep things clear. Yet, at times I got technical and used jargon. For some, I may seem simplistic.

For all these short-comings I apologize. Decisions had to be made and I made what I felt was best.

My intentions are to revise and update this book every year to include new advances in Internet technology. Your insights are valuable to me. If you have any questions or comments feel free to write me at my publishing company.

During the Dark Ages it was common to write an apology for anything you wrote to keep the church appeased when a controversial topic was covered. An apology could be a page or carry on for a hundred pages or more. I know that a reader may enjoy watching the author struggle with his keyboard. But I am only going to apologize for a page.

I want to thank several people for their valuable help. My wife, Sue, has the patience of a Saint. She puts up with a lot from me when I write. I thank Sue for her kindness and patience and love. My assistant and Copy Editor, Julie Ledger, never wavered as the project neared completion. Joyfully she reached forward and kept the office alive while I buried myself in research and writing.

Special thanks goes to all my attorneys, including, Chris Sitzmann, Mary Lou Robinson, and Kevin Musolf. All the unsung heroes that run the ACLU Website deserve a round of applause.

Countless others have lent a hand in my work. Thank you, everyone, where ever you are.

Table of Contents

Introduction

An ominous knock at the door awakens you from a nice afternoon nap. You look out the window to see who could be so rude as to disturb you on a sunny summer afternoon. And then you see it is the police.

You open the door as your heart begins to race. Has someone been in a car accident? Has a family member died?

After a short talk with the police you learn that your worst nightmare has just come true. Your twelve-year-old son, the one that gets straight A's in school, has been sending pornography to his friends over the Internet. You also learn that your fourteen-year-old daughter has been in close contact with a thirty eight-year old man three states away.

To make the nightmare worse, you are arrested for possession of child pornography, the pornography your son downloaded into your computer.

After spending $30,000 of your hard-earned money defending yourself in court, you are relieved that you are found innocent. Unfortunately, your name has been dragged through the mud and your neighbors no longer even look at you (you made the front page of your local newspaper).

Your son ends up on probation, which is another added expense for you, and your son now has a felony conviction on his criminal record. Fortunately, the thirty eight-year-old man was arrested before he could make physical contact with your daughter. Good thing she never got the bus tickets he was about to send her to visit him.

The above short story could easily be you. The Internet is entering every area of our lives and is expected to continue to grow at a fast pace until over 90% of all households are on the Internet.

Your children will be on the Internet with friends and at school whether you know how to use a computer or not.

This book is designed to help parents protect and monitor their children in their Internet activities. You do not need to be a computer expert to use this book. Rather, everything in this book has been put in very simple, easy to use format. Advanced computer users will find this book of great value too, as I will give several short cuts to limiting your children's activities in certain areas of the Internet.

Step-by-step I will show you how to find hidden files on your computer, especially photographs. I will show you how to find out where your children have been online. And finally, I will outline how to protect yourself from accusations of Internet crime.

Seldom does a day go by without a news article of lives destroyed from some infraction involving the Internet. Protecting your family is of the greatest importance. It is not difficult to regulate what your children watch on TV. Just restrict use or don't have access to pay-for-view channels and other such channels. The Internet is not so easy to regulate. Most of the time your children will be on the Internet without you looking over their shoulder. And most people do not sit down in the living room and watch the Internet like television. Usually, your children will view the Internet alone and in private, even at a friend's home or at school.

While you think your son is doing research for a school project he could be surfing the worst types of pornography in newsgroups, pornography that includes torture, bondage, bestiality, child pornography and more. Your daughter could be in a chat room talking with a pedophile.

There you have it: The greatest tool ever in the history of mankind can be the greatest blessing or worst nightmare. The Internet is information. Knowledge is power. How safely your family uses the Internet will largely depend on how much knowledge you have of the basic workings of the Internet.

Chapter 1

Makeup of the Internet

Before we can begin we need to take a brief look at how and why the Internet is made up the way it is.

The Internet had its origins in 1969 in an experimental program called the Advanced Research Project Agency (ARPA), also called ARPANET. The idea was to connect the military with defense contractors and university labs involved in military research.

The main focus of ARPANET was to put together a decentralized computer network that had ample redundant computer back-up links. It was hoped that this system could provide rapid communication transmission without human control. The goal was to keep the flow of information moving in the event of an all out war, especially nuclear.

As time went on, this new system, ARPANET, evolved beyond its original intent. Eventually, corporations and individuals became involved with ARPANET, which began to be called DARPA Internet, and then just, the Internet.

No single company or person controls or administers the Internet. That is why it is so difficult for the government to regulate the Internet. If you change the laws in one country, the person posting information to the net just sets up shop in a country that allows the activity in question.

And with the millions of people on the Internet each day, how could the government possibly police every activity on the net. They can't. That is why you must, as a parent, understand the fundamentals of the Internet to protect yourself and your children.

World Wide Web

The World Wide Web is what we hear about most often in the news these days. However, this is only one part of the Web.

The World Wide Web is made up of Websites. Corporations, universities, organizations, and individuals have set up their own Websites. The information on a Website covers just about anything. There are hundreds of thousands of different Websites covering topics from snails, buying a home, books, travel information and pornography. There are thousands of different subjects.

You or your children can do research for school or college, surf the net for interesting or fun things, or get in trouble.

The World Wide Web is the newest part of the Internet and offers the easiest and best access. Websites are user-friendly, even for the novice. In most cases you just point your mouse and click. You do not need any fancy or hi-tech knowledge to surf.

Most of what you find on the World Wide Web is useful, entertaining, interesting or harmless. However, a portion of the World Wide Web contains pornography. The good news is that the worst porn is actually in the newsgroups. And even better news: The pornographic sites on the World Wide Web are usually restricted to adults that will pay by credit card to enter. This provides a small natural barrier to entrance by children.

The bad news is that most of these porn Web Sites have a cover page that can be as bad as anything found in adult men's magazines. I assume there is even worse material inside these pornographic Websites. Later in this book I will show you how to make it tough for your children to go to these areas and I'll also show you how to find out if your children have been to these types of sites in the recent past.

Porn Websites are getting to be big business. Recently, the Wall Street Journal had an article on how celebrities invested in the set-up of Websites of a pornographic nature. It seems that this is the most profitable business on the World Wide Web today.

If that isn't enough, the worst kind of operators set-up overseas where laws are lax or nonexistent. Child pornography runs rampant from many of these areas. Frequently, you will find oriental pornography of very young girls. They claim that any child twelve or older in Japan is free game. I am not sure of the truth of this, but regardless of the laws, young children, male and female, end up in compromising positions on the Internet.

What I want to make clear at this point is that I am not totally against pornography. What an adult wishes to view privately is their own concern, however, children need to be restricted from these kinds of material until they are mature enough to handle the content. I am against several types of pornography that exists on the Internet. Pornography containing torture, rape, children, bestiality (humans with animals), bondage, and homosexuality, go beyond what I feel is appropriate, even if it is legal material.

I say this because certain types of pornography can easily get out of control. An example: Some time ago, while surfing the Internet I ran across a picture so disgusting it actually etched my mind and remains a vivid picture after all these years. The picture was of a human (I could not tell the gender), cut up and torn, lying in a pile. The poster claimed to be a serial killer and the picture of a victim. The body appeared to be dead for several days as the body was all purple and you could actually see flies on the body.

This is an example of what I mean by unacceptable pornography. This picture had no redeeming value. It was not erotic, could not be a marital aid, and could not be considered artistic. The picture was sadism.

My goal is not to prevent adults from running across these types of pictures. My goal is to give you the tools so your children don't run across these kinds of pictures, if not for the effect on the mind, then to keep as much distance between your children and these kinds of people.

A Website can be set-up by anyone. In fact a Website can be a lot of fun for the whole family. For around $2,000 anyone can have a modest Website, from your church to yourself.

And the Internet has grown significantly in recent years. In 1981, less than 300 computer were connected to the Internet. In 1989, more than 90,000 computers were connected. In 1993, over 1 million computers were Internet connected. Today, it is estimated that nearly 10 million computers are linked to the Internet, of which 60% are estimated to be here in the United States.

It is impossible to be exact, but it is estimated that 40 million people worldwide have access to the Internet. It is estimated that by 1999 over 200 million computers will be connected to the Internet.

The Internet is growing and evolving. Efforts by the government and local law enforcement are inadequate. Only you, as a parent, can provide a sufficient framework for your children to work within.

Newsgroups

Newsgroups are one of the more interesting areas of the Internet. Newsgroups are unregulated forums. Frequently, the poster of a message or file is anonymous. It is simple for the poster to cover his tracks and leave no trail. That is the main reason why illegal and questionable activity in this area of the Internet goes on unchallenged.

Newsgroups are very different from Websites. Your children can get in real serious trouble here. Pornography of the worst kind and on hundreds of subjects resides in this part of the Internet.

Web Sites allow you to just point your mouse and click. In Newsgroups you need a little more knowledge of the Net and how it works to function here. The best way to learn is to experiment, your children certainly will.

A newsgroup does not have a pretty picture to show you all your options. Rather, everything is in text form here, even the pictures. In a newsgroup you receive pictures (and sounds, and movies) in the form of what looks like 'junk letters'. You then run these junk letters through a decoder (UUDECODE) and then view the picture with a special viewer.

Newer computers have this built right in. Sometimes you don't even have to download anything;

the picture is decoded automatically and appears on your screen as your computer receives it. If you don't save the picture, it will not be on your computer.

Depending on your computer, you may need to download some or most pictures in the form of 'junk letters', decode, and then view them. This can lead to some problems. In some places it is illegal to even possess certain types of pictures. Child pornography is a bad thing to even have in your computer, whether you produced the picture or not.

Movies can also be downloaded from newsgroups (as well as Websites). Movies have to be downloaded to your computer and decoded before they will work. You also will not know what the movie contains until you download and decode the entire file. This can be time consuming. One note: It is expected that with the new hi-speed modems coming out in late 1998 or early 1999 that movies will be available in real time. This means that instead of taking hours in some cases to download a movie, you could download an entire movie in a matter of minutes.

Now I would like to share some facts about newsgroups. Currently, the Internet contains some fifteen thousand different newsgroup topics. Over 100,000 new messages are added each day to these newsgroups. Between a third and half of all messages posted to newsgroups would be considered inappropriate by most parents.

Newsgroups, however, offer some very exciting ways to communicate large volumes of information.

If you are doing a research project for school or personal reasons that requires large files to be transferred, including pictures, movies or sounds, between a large number of people, newsgroups are the best way to go.

An example: Let's say you are interested in pictures taken by the Hubble telescope and all related information. You could try to stay in touch by e-mail, and for some personal inquiries you probably would. But, to keep up to date with a variety of scientists you could frequent a newsgroup on the Hubble telescope. You could also receive picture in binary form (remember those 'junk letters' that you need to decode and then view). You or your children could do a up-to-date report for school or for any personal reason just by stopping by a newsgroup.

You could do the same thing to put together a family tree with people across the United States. You may even wish to start your own newsgroup.

With something so good come challenges. Some less than honorable people travel the Internet newsgroups, working to seduce children. Your child is their target. They offer games and pictures that arouse the curiosity of adults and children. As an adult you can make a good decision. Children, in their innocent desire to learn, are more easily convinced.

Rather than looking at pictures of deep space from the Hubble telescope or from the Mars Pathfinder, pornography of all kinds is offered. Later in this book I will outline some of the hundreds of sex topics the newsgroups offer.

America Online

Several commercial Internet and quasi-internet services exist. However, America Online (AOL) is the largest and fastest growing. AOL has a commanding lead over CompuServe and other such services and I feel AOL will continue their commanding lead. Therefore, I will focus on AOL in this discussion.

No book on the Internet would be complete without talking in-depth about AOL and the services they offer. AOL can be the safest place for your children to play when it comes to the Internet, but it is by no means risk-free.

America Online actually has areas just for kids. Games dominate this area, but other things can be done there, too. Keep in mind, anyone, even pedophiles, can enter these 'kids areas'.

AOL also has a built in parental control. However, you must set up the parental controls and they are not fail-safe.

If you desire ease of use with massive content, AOL is the way to go. The variety of subjects is large. They include: Stock and business information, weather, e-mail, research, entertainment, news, online help, sports, travel, clubs, education, reference, marketplace, and more. You can read from several newspapers around the country for the cost of your regular AOL service. You can also download freeware (computer programs, including games, that are free for you to use), shareware (programs and games that you can try before you buy), and demos (a scaled down version of an over-the-counter program).

America Online is not technically the Internet. AOL has its own vast universe of content that they generally control. However, you can get access to the Internet through AOL, including both newsgroups and Websites.

AOL parental controls do allow for some limitations to be placed on your children, but you need to set the controls up and the controls are relatively easy to circumvent.

Before we move on to the next chapter we need to review a very popular toy on America Online called Chat Rooms. They offer entertainment for you and your children, but contain some of the riskiest Internet elements.

Chat Rooms

Chat Rooms are popping up all over the place on the Internet. America Online contains some of the most popular and easiest to use. Chat Rooms are also showing up on other Internet Websites.

Chat Rooms can vary from site to site, but they have one underlying theme. All Chat Rooms are real time gathering places where people can talk on a variety of subjects.

If you don't like the kinds of topics covered by the standard Chat Rooms, you can create your own.

Chat Rooms on Websites outside AOL and other mainstream Internet providers can be lax in their regulating of content. Some Websites have no controls and an anything goes attitude, kind of like a Jerry Springer talk show on the Internet without any bodyguards to step in when things get wild. Children frequently have free and easy access to these types of sites.

I will focus on AOL Chat Rooms here, as they are the most widely used. AOL does monitor their Chat Rooms. If someone creates a new Chat Room that is questionable they can shut it down after the very short time it takes them to realize the Chat Room has been created. AOL generally will allow most Chat

Rooms as long as they do not encourage children with sex, dirty talk, or pornography.

One thing to keep in mind, Chat Rooms seldom stay on topic in the general areas. For example: A Chat Room called *Friends First* could quickly turn to vulgarity and come-ons toward female chatters. The Chat Room monitor can quickly stop things if they get too far out of hand, however, there is not a monitor in all rooms at all times.

Unfortunately, Chat Rooms can go semi-private. If a sexual predator in a Chat Room sees a young girl there he may approach her with an Instant Message. This allows for a private conversation between the two people involved, no monitor. If your child is the target, an Instant Message from the predator will appear on your child's computer screen. Your child will have no information on who sent the Instant Message except what the sender wants your child to see.

The sender of the message probably used your child's profile to determine if it is worth the effort to approach your child.

A profile is a screen you or your child can set up letting people know some basic and even personal information about you. I recommend that you never set up a profile on yourself or your children. Anyone can view these profiles without your consent.

If you do want to set up a profile never give out your real name, address, and phone number, marital status, or age. You can include your online name, a favorite quote, generic hobbies or interests, or the state you live in. Do not even go as far as to put your city down.

Keep in mind that if you decide to create a profile, even a very generic one, programs putting together mailing lists will easily find your e-mail address and use it to market to you. Once you are on a mailing list you will get piles of junk e-mail called SPAM. A vast majority of SPAM contains offers of sex, pornography, sexual Website link-ups, cable TV converter boxes (illegal in many instances), offers to sell products using SPAM, and hot stocks tips (tips that are not really so hot).

Chat Rooms, in my opinion, are dangerous. The talk that goes on in these Chat Rooms is usually empty talk and usually ends up as stupid talk. Chat Rooms are generally a waste of time. I encourage parents to keep their children away from Chat Rooms. With Chat Room names on America Online like, Gay, Lesbian, First Date, Friends First, Chance Encounters, The Flirts Nook, and Hey Girlfriend, children should be kept away. Trouble awaits young people bored that happen to stumble into a Chat Room. The pedophiles and stalkers feed on these children.

The best advice, surf the Internet and AOL with your children. Use parental controls whenever possible. And most of all talk to your children about the Internet. See what they see. You raise your children to look both ways before crossing the street and to never talk to strangers. They need to look before they enter a Web Site and never talk to strangers on the Internet either. And make your children understand that they must never give out personal information over the Internet. No matter what!

Chapter 2

Where Internet Indecencies Reside

"We live in a sick society," a neighbor of mine stated.

He was referring to how we have become pornophobic in our society today. In the past you could take a picture of your child in the bathtub, today you could find yourself in court over the same thing. What a parent considers cute, the district attorney may consider a felony.

Even if a photographed child is clothed, it could still be considered pornographic by some.

Today's laws take the most beautiful thing in the world, your child entering this world, and make it a vulgar crime by recording the event. It makes one wonder if we need to rewrite history. My most vivid picture of the Vietnam War is a photo of a girl about ten-years-old running toward the camera naked, dirty and crying. Do we change the history books to satisfy the censors?

Why is society so pornophobic? There are good reasons. Children are abused, tortured, and raped at ever increasing rates. Parents are alarmed and with good reason. Appendix One is an outline of just how many pornographic newsgroups there are and I would provide a list of Websites, but they number in the tens of thousands.

I want to outline just a few of the ways our attitudes in society have changed about sex, marriage, and children. Then I will show you some examples of why.

In the recent past it was common for girls to get married at a very young age, sometimes as young as twelve. Boys married young, too, but usually a little older. Many girls, still children by today's standards, had children of their own by age thirteen and fourteen. Maybe your parents or grandparents fall into this group.

Recently, in my local newspaper, *The Post-Crescent*, an article was run on the longest married couple in the United States. I believe the article was nationally run as well. The article stated that this couple got married some 80 years ago. He was twenty-two, she was twelve. They had their first child a year later. The article praised how wonderful it was that this lovely couple has weathered over 80 years together. And they are still in love.

A few days later a letter to the editor was printed. The writer stated that if this lovely couple tried to do today what they did over 80 years ago he would have been branded a sexual predator and she a poor victim. Times have changed, human nature has not.

I recall this story from memory, but the facts are representational. The letter to the editor was correct. The twenty-two year old man would have been tossed into prison for such a heinous act. I do not believe that this man felt himself to be a pervert, nor his children. They appeared to be well-adjusted, kind, and loving parents.

Keep in mind that 80 years ago things were much different. Society has changed and so have our attitudes and needs. People live longer and don't need to get married so young. Not only is the length of their marriage a miracle, so is their biological age. The man was over age 100 when most people born in his day made it into the 50's at best.

That does not change the fact that 2 billion years of human evolution can be denied. Man has survived for the same reason any species survives, it has propagates itself. People are interested in sex. It is a normal curiosity. However, in our modern society, we find children as victims of rape, incest, torture, white slavery, and worse. We cannot stop children from thinking about sex once they hit puberty. But we, as parents, have the responsibility to educate our children. On the Internet children are fair game to pedophiles.

I want to share one more story that I think will illustrate a point.

Frequently, we hear that early age marriages in the past were a result of out agrarian society. That is not totally true. Great minds of the recent past also married young.

Take, for example, the grand careers of Will and Ariel Durant. Over their life they created what can easily be called the greatest compilation of integral history. Integral history is the unique way of looking at history that focuses on the people, art, philosophy, religion, politics, literature and lifestyle of a culture. Will and Ariel Durant provided us with the most complete integral history of Western civilization. Their eleven volume *Story of Civilization* series covers Western Civilization from the beginning to Napoleon. Over 10,000 pages and a lifetime are consumed. They spent eight to fourteen hours every day on this grand work starting in 1927 and continuing until the late 1970's. I recommend that everyone find the time to read their work. It is available in most bookstores. Serious minds read serious work. A lifetime of experience and study come together in this work and is a must read.

The Durant name may not be legend, but they are among the greatest minds of the 20th century. Yet, even great minds of the very recent past would be considered perverted in the society of today.

Will Durant was born in 1885. He met his future wife as one of his students (yes, he was a teacher), and later married her at the age of 15. He was twenty-eight when he got married, thirteen years older. He resigned from the school to marry his love.

Thirteen years later he met with great success with his book *The Story of Philosophy*. This allowed him to retire from teaching and start *The Story of Civilization* series of books that would occupy the remaining 54 years of his life.

Was Will Durant a pervert? Was his wife, Ariel, a victim? No, on both counts. After 67 years of marriage, Ariel Durant died, at the age of 83. Will Durant, heart-broken with grief, died 13 days later at the age of 96.

I would argue that Will and Ariel were much in love. Their life work is a valuable part of our culture and a valued addition to out repository of knowledge.

So why does our current society discourage this type of activity now? Why, when a female teacher courts a mid-teens male student and has a child with him does society gasp in horror? Is it really wrong when society goes off half-cocked when a teacher has a sexual relationship with a student?

The teacher referred to above made national news. She even had contact with the *boy* after the court ordered her not too. Is society out of control? Should we really be worried when young people have sex with other young people? Or girls having a sexual relationship with older men?

I believe the answer is yes. In the past things *were* different. Will Durant did resign to marry his love, a student.

More important, it is not love or sex that motivates many pedophiles today. Frequently, these children are abused, tortured, used to generate money for the sex industry, or killed.

The local news media reported several months ago of a fifteen-year-old girl from Sturgeon Bay, Wisconsin, a small town in the finger of the state that met a man on the Internet. This man told the girl that he was about her age. He convinced her that they should get together and sent her a bus ticket to meet him in Milwaukee. When the girl saw the man she realized he was much older and ran away. It was discovered that the man was from Florida and thirty-eight.

What intentions did this thirty-eight year old man have with a fifteen-year-old girl? I doubt they were totally honorable.

What would have happened if this man had gotten close enough to grab the girl or was more violent? This girl would have become another statistic or she would never have been heard from or seen again.

Where were the police? They had no idea of what was happening. The girl's parents informed the police and the man was later apprehended.

Where were the parents? Don't they care about their little girl? The truth is that the parents cared a lot for their little girl. The parents did not know that their daughter was having a serious relationship with a thirty-eight year old Florida man. How could the parents have prevented this near tragedy? A few simple steps that I will outline could have tipped off the parents into their daughter's activities. The police cannot protect your children. Only you can monitor and supervise your children effectively.

The sad truth is that all children are at risk. Boys are in as high demand as girls. Don't think you can let your son do as he pleases while you keep a tight rein on your daughter. If you surf the netherworld parts of the Internet you will understand what I mean. The abuse of boys is just as great for boys as with girls. For the remainder of this chapter we will discuss these darker areas of the Internet.

Websites

There are an estimated 16,000 pornographic Websites as I write this and the number is expected to double every nine months. Pornographic Web Sites are among the more profitable areas on the Net.

Just where are these Websites that you would rather your children stay away from?

They are not hard to find. Go to any search engine and begin a research project. Some of the seemingly most innocent topics will lead you to the darker side of the Net.

You can use Websites to browse or do research or both. The best way to find Websites of interest is by using a Search Engine, such as, Yahoo, Infoseek, NetFind, HotBot, or Dogpile. Just add *.com* after the search engine name and there you go. Most Internet services take you to a random search engine just by clicking *Search.* America Online uses NetFind, for example.

A simple and innocent research project your children need to do for school can quickly get them into trouble. Curiosity requires it.

I am now going to cover several simple Search examples that bring pornography straight to your children.

As an example, let us say that your daughter has a school project to research a favorite career. Your daughter decides on nursing. She goes to the Internet and does a search. She types in *nurse* and hits enter. Here is what she gets.

The Search Engine at AOL, NetFind, finds that the first and most relevant Web Site begins with "*hot nurse all day long*". The description goes on to say, "*Click Here for free pics I knew hot nurse couldn't take pornstar more of this...*". Even though the grammar is bad, there is no doubt what is going on here.

The second entry has a heading, "*nurse lolitas all day long*". Lolitas frequently refers to young children. When you see words like Lolita or Lollitot, what is being sold is children. Lollitot has two parts. The *tot* part stands for a child. The *loli* stands for lollipop. The insinuation is that children are good enough to eat. I ran across some sad humor as I researched this. An individual that bragged about his pedophilia stated, "Of course, I like children. They taste like chicken." If it were not so sad one could maybe turn a slight smile.

The third entry is also pornographic. The fourth entry is about teenage nurse girls. In fact, all ten hits were pornographic. Not one single hit would have been of value to your child's school research project. When you do a search you generally get ten hits (Websites) to go to. You can get the next ten if you continue, and so forth.

If your daughter just clicked on the first entry she would have been greeted by pornography as bad as is found in adult men's magazines. If your daughter paid to enter the site there would have been worse.

You may say, "But nursing is a female occupation. You have to expect some of this." Well, for one, nursing is not just a female occupation. And, regardless, I doubt that the first most relevant hits had to be pornographic.

So your daughter is done with her schoolwork and your son sits down at the PC and logs in. His school project is on money so he enters that into the Search Engine and here is what he gets.

The first two hits are on stocks, not bad. But number three looks a little odd. It reads, "*Money – Hardcore Sex*". Number nine is similar saying, "*WILD THINGS 3 electronic money books electronic money*". Not too bad. But it continues, "*With each lick, she slid her fingers inside her own electronic money wet ^%&$@...*".

The money search did better with eight out of ten non-pornographic. Yet, it is concerning that something as innocent as money could yield two such results.

Now your daughter is back at the computer. She has joined cheerleading. You can imagine what that search resulted in. Cheerleaders resulted in all ten hits being pornographic.

Now you, as a parent, take a seat. You are planning a trip to Japan or France. Both searches resulted in five out of ten hits being pornographic, not the exact thing you planned for the trip.

What I am pointing out here is how easy it is to find indecent material on the Web. You don't have to look hard.

If your daughter is at the age when she enjoys dolls, she may wish to look up the American Girl Doll Company. If she types in the entire name she is ok. If she cuts the search to American Girl, she will have her eyes full. And heaven forbid that your children would ever become serious and type *sex* into the search Engine.

The good news is that entry into these Websites is restricted. To enter you need to prove your age with a verification that usually requires a credit card. The bad news is that the front page to pornographic Websites is not something you probably want your children to see.

Parental Controls offer some help and I will cover them more fully in Chapter Three. There are several kinds available over the counter. However, I will focus on the Parental Controls of America Online in this book. If you use the Netscape Navigator or Microsoft Explorer browser you can get programs like NetNanny.

Before I go any further I want to explain the focus of the early part of this discussion. It may seem like I am working up fear in you. And that is precisely the point.

Advertisers know how to sell things best. The best commercials first get you to feel some pain. Maybe you have an unquenchable thirst or you are made to feel guilty for not calling home for a while. Then the advertiser gives you a pleasurable solution. Drink our brand of soft drink or call home with our long distance company and all will be well. In that regard this entire book is a walking billboard. I want you to be aware of what exists on the Internet, especially the bad. I'm not a negative person, but I have to paint the picture so you understand and are motivated to take action.

Frequently, I am told when a discussion on the Internet comes up that the pornography on the Internet is just like you will find in a popular over the counter adult men's magazine. Nothing could be further from the truth. Some is quite mild, others very perverse. And it is common to see people attempt to solicit others, especially children, into these perverse sex acts that include child pornography, bestiality, torture, prostitution, bondage, homosexual relations, and more.

I will be outlining the worst area of the Net next. I personally feel that every parent ought to see first hand what I am talking about. It will provide the motivation to take real action, put restrictions on what your children can see and do online.

Before you examine these wayward newsgroups you should talk with your attorney. The laws vary from area to area. Prudence is always best.

Newsgroups

If Websites offer pornography it probably tends toward that which is available in most communities and is similar to what is found in popular adult men's magazines. You may find it disturbing, but it is by far the more mild forms of pornography.

Newsgroups on the other hand are not so tame. The worst indecencies reside here. Newsgroups by their very nature are unregulated and anonymous. Providing personal information over a newsgroup is done at your own risk.

Newsgroups are not the Internet, but use the Internet to transfer information. You may hear newsgroups referred to as UseNet from time to time. UseNet stands for User's Network and is the same thing as a newsgroup.

In Appendix One I listed all the newsgroups that advertise that they provide pornographic pictures. The list is extensive, but not all-inclusive. For example, Appendix One lists all newsgroups under the *alt.binaries.pictures.erotic* news threads. However, there are newsgroups with titles like *sex, erotica* and *pictures*.

Not all pictures are listed under the *alt.binaries.pictures* area. The *alt* stands for alternative newsgroups. The *binaries* stands for the way files (pictures) are transmitted in code.

Generally, newsgroups are on topic. That is, the information in the newsgroup is what its title says. This is not always true but newsgroups that are set up to offer discussion about sex with no pictures can in fact have picture files attached.

Here I will provide some examples from Appendix One of the types of pornographic newsgroups available and the number of postings to the newsgroup.

Some pornographic newsgroups are general in nature. They include topics like *centerfolds, black, asian, latino, legs, Marti-gras, pornstar,* and *redheads.* Even though the newsgroup heading sounds similar to over the counter adult men's magazines, they sometimes contain additional, off-topic, pornography.

The tendency is toward the young, both boys and girls. The people that post to these newsgroups work very hard to make legal adults look very young. Frequently, morphing is used. Morphing is where a picture is modified on the computer using special programs so the picture looks like something totally different. With morphing, a woman can be significantly modified until she looks very young, possible early-teens or slightly younger.

Morphed pictures look very real. Some are done poorly and are obvious. However, if a picture appears to be a young girl it has doubtful value. The old porn industry adage that pornography is used as a marital aid holds no water if the picture is a morph depicting a child in a lewd act.

If your children, out of curiosity, discover these newsgroups, significant harm could be done to their development. Children are impressionable. When they see these kinds of pictures they get a false impression of reality. Boys tend more than girls to express curiosity in pornography. A young boy exposed to these types of pictures could later get involved with a girl and react with her in a negative way. I try to phrase this in a politically correct way, but the reality is blunt. Children learn by example. Pornographic newsgroups offer poor examples. As adults we can make conscious decisions of what is right and wrong, whereas, children are developing their consciousness, values, and morals.

How hard is it to find the newsgroups listed in Appendix One? Not very hard at all. Most Internet servers, including America Online, will give you a complete list of all newsgroups. All you need is a little time to review which newsgroups you find interesting and subscribe to them.

I make it easy for parents to find where pornography in newsgroups resides with Appendix One. My goal is to get this into parent's hands, not children's. Yes, children could, with this book, find pornography. The sad fact is that many children already know where it is and if they don't their friends do. It is easy for children to find this information and children have the time to surf the Internet to get what they want. It is a big game.

Parents, on the other hand, don't always know these things. Parents also don't always have the time to learn what their children know about the computer. Therefore, I provide a shortcut. You, as a parent, can use this book to see what is out there first-hand and decide what you want your children to have access too.

Let me give you some examples of what you will find in the newsgroup heading *alt.binaries.pictures.erotica.*

Every taste is covered. There are newsgroups for people interested in seeing *bestiality, bondage, biker-chicks, breasts.small* or *breasts.saggy, cartoons, centerfolds, child, children, disney, early-teens, facials, fetish, fisting, girlfriends, groupsex, gymnast-girls, high-school, lesbians, male.anal, olderman, pornstar, pre-teens, pregnant, rape, tasteless, torture, transvestites, upskirt, violence, voyeurism,* and *young.* Even an ACLU attorney will have his stomach turned over this soup of smut.

But the numbers really bring fear to the hearts of parents. Under *bestiality* there were 1,711 postings the day I checked. *Early-teens* had 2,047 postings, *facials* had 1,664, *gaymen* listed 3,104, *pre-teen* showed 2,697 postings, and *teen.male* offered 2,084 postings.

Newsgroups like *girlfriends* encourage people to take a picture of their girlfriend or wife and get revenge if they ever leave you by posting the picture online. The *disney* newsgroup shows pictures of Disney cartoon characters in ways you would not expect to see at the movie theater. I am sure Disney would like to stop these pornographic pictures of Ariel from *The Little Mermaid* or Jasmine from *Aladdin.* But newsgroups, remember, are anonymous.

Newsgroups can encourage bad behavior. The *rape* newsgroup encourages viewers to record their rape in progress and share this with the general audience of the newsgroup.

Considering this, prevention is key. Parental controls offer modest help and I will discuss them more fully in Chapter Three. The best thing any parent can do is keep their children away from these dark areas of the Internet. It is only a matter of time before your child will be targeted as a victim if they roam free in these kinds of areas.

Chat Rooms

Chat Rooms cause me more concern than even newsgroups. Personally, I find Chat Rooms to have little value and are an open invitation to stalk and victimize women and children.

Don't get me wrong, there are some good Chat Rooms. America Online has a *Writer's* Chat Room that I find very informative, entertaining, and sociable. I even met Tom Clancy there several times and enjoyed good conversation with him.

However, many of the general Chat Rooms denigrate to age and sex checks, personal information swaps, and offers of pornographic pictures.

Appendix Two contains several examples I recorded from AOL Chat Rooms. This offers a good cross-section of the material exchanged in general Chat Rooms.

Chat Rooms are often filled with young people from the age of twelve to age twenty-five. Personal information is encouraged to be shared.

I will now take some examples from Appendix Two of the type of behavior to be avoided in a Chat Room as well as some smart moves. What I want to avoid is a technical discussion. Another book can teach you how to use your computer, this book will outline the risks of the Internet and how to set up protections and monitor your children's activities online.

It does not take long to see that a similar theme develops in most Chat Rooms. People are curious about who they are talking with which leads to an exchange of personal information in a very public forum. Casual watchers can also see and use this information.

One of the most frequent refrains is:

age/sex check.

Several people reply with:

22/f

or:

28/m

or some other similar type of response.

The *22/f* is simple to understand. First the age is listed and then the sex.

Quickly, more personal information is requested. In example number one, Play4PGA asks:

any ladies wanna chat?

BUDICE32 lets everyone know that

i have a son 7 months old

And then says:

oh I guess your not married.

Then pornographic solicitations begin. GRVLTRVL makes his entrance with:

hello all 24/m/pic here.

GRVLTRVL is advertising that he is a twenty-four year old male with pictures either of himself or others.

MARLMANI quickly adds:

hello ladies any females want to private chat?

Andimat immediately responds:

I would love to private chat.

Private chat can be a couple of different things. First, it could be that a private Chat Room has been set up and only people with correct pass-code can get in, or, an Instant Message conversation can be set up. An Instant Message is a private conversation between two people.

Frequently, Instant Messages are used to get one-on-one with someone to acquire personal information. This is not always the case, but it can be. The situation is one where your young children should not be involved.

Ghosts are also a concern. People in a Chat Room virtually always use an online name that does not disclose who they are. You can set up your online profile as anyone you like. You could say you are a twenty year old female living in New York when in fact you are a forty year old man living in Florida and no one would know unless you told them.

It is common for men to display themselves as a female to get attention from other males. A ghost displayed as a mid-teens female would get plenty of attention from the young males as well as the pedophiles. This would be the perfect come-on to sell pornography or stalk a child.

The real problem comes in when a real mid-teens girl sets up online. They become the focus of much unwanted attention. They will be made several offers for pornography and offers to *cyber*.

When you review Appendix Two you will notice that periodically someone will make an offer to *cyber*. What this means is that they want to get together with an Instant Message one-on-one and talk dirty, similar to phone sex that is advertised on late-night television, except this in done over the computer in text. This can lead to the passing of personal information that could put your child in serious risk. Neither your child, nor you as the parent, have any secure way of knowing who is on the other side of the conversation. It could be two youngsters experimenting or a pedophile on the make. As always, my advice is to keep your children away from this sort of thing. Make sure your children know your concerns and how easy it would be to get hurt.

There are other more subtle ways to say the same thing. Again, in Appendix Two, Example One, Danimal476 asks:

anyone want to chat? IM me.

IM stands for Instant Message and Danimal476 is really asking to *cyber*. Several young girls in Example One also admit that they are babysitting. Even if no other information is given out it is best not to disclose such information. It is possible in some cases to learn the identity of someone online without their consent or their providing information. The Internet has massive information resources that can be used to find the identity and location of an individual. The work involved to do this is extensive, but it is best to be safe than sorry.

Sometimes, a wise Chat Room user will respond:

?/m,

thereby not disclosing his age, just his gender. That is probably the safest way to go. However, any female that wanders into a Chat Room becomes fair game, at any age.

One final excerpt from Example One in Appendix Two. Some souls are quite forward and blunt when they are interested in getting a young girl to *cyber*. Madforker states matter-of-factly:

any f wanna teach me to CYBER im me

I know that for most people Appendix Two is [illegible], but that is the way things are done in [illegible] Quickly, you will realize that the entire premise of many Chat Rooms is come-ons toward girls. Chat Room users can bluntly say they are interested in teenage girls.

America Online does monitor Chat Rooms, but not all rooms at all times. AOL frequently relies on other members to keep them informed of Terms of Membership violations. Even if AOL cancels an account, the user can log on later with a new account and as a new member. And then they are back in business.

How They Hook Your Children

Appendix Three has got to rank as the highest nightmare any parent could imagine. Here I show you how pedophiles target your children in an organized and anonymous way.

I used real postings from several newsgroups listed in Appendix One. I focused on active newsgroups that cater toward child pornography. Review Appendix Three now and then we can continue this discussion.

Now that you reviewed the contents of Appendix Three I would like to make a few comments starting with Example Number One.

It is hard to decide which example is the worst; they all raise serious concerns. Example One is from someone claiming to be a fourteen-year-old female babysitter. This babysitter is requesting information on how to molest the children she is entrusted to care for.

This has got to rank about as high as you can go for concerns parents have. My wife and I first checked out the babysitters that we use to take care of our child. We were fortunate enough to find someone through our church. However, there is no guarantee that even someone from church will be reliable. This first posting scares the daylight out of me. All I can recommend is to check the references of any babysitter you use. And pray it is not the person that posted example Number One.

Example Number One is listed by someone *claiming* to be a fourteen-year-old girl. It could be anyone, even a ghost. The person on the other side could be a law enforcement person involved in a sting operation. However, it is more likely an adult hunting for prey.

Example Number Two is a complaint that someone posted pictures of girls too old. He complains that the pictures are of girls that are in their early teens and that he prefers pre-teens.

The third example is probably the most disturbing. This posting is a recruitment effort. The qualifications to enter the so-called Pedo University require that the person applying provide a certain amount of child pornography to the newsgroup. The posting goes on to say that nudity is not required and that the pictures do not have to be original and that, "Pedo U does NOT demand or incite the posting of illegal material".

Then a full listing of all staff members are included that go on for pages. Even though the poster claims not to "incite the posting of illegal material" that is exactly what he is doing.

The newsgroup on *pre-teens* even has a Website dedicated toward helping the pedophile stay ahead of the authorities. For an eye opening experience you can visit this Website at:

www.abpep-t.home.ml.org

What concerns me the most is that the effort to exploit children is an organized effort. Many of the postings are about the difficulties these pedophiles have in real life around children. The younger the better is their mantra.

I have viewed serious amounts of material for this book. One thing struck me quickly as I reviewed the material in these newsgroups is that the children, mostly young girls, never look happy about the situation they are in. One can only guess what events lead them to this.

Sometimes someone will post an angry message in an attempt to slow this behavior down. It never works. It only seems to encourage the pedophile community. Example Number Seven is a good example of this. The response back is pointed as you can see from Example Number Eight, where the poster claims all computer and Internet bigwigs are really hackers and pedophiles. Example Eight even goes as far as to brag that the FBI and Congress know this and condone it because they are powerless to do anything about it; besides, they are all pedophiles, too. Most computer users and Internet surfers are not pedophiles, but the criminal mind needs the illusion.

And finally, Example Number Ten is an example of an individual trying to get someone involves in bestiality. Just when you thought it could not get any more disgusting, they move to a lower level.

Pornography and other indecencies reside in all corners of the Internet. Even America Online, which does monitor a large part of the activity on their system, has risks. No place is completely safe, but that is real life, too.

We see things on the evening news that causes us serious concern. We are moved to action when the headlines show another victim. Then, as the memory fades, we get lax. That is what the pedophiles and stalkers count on. You cannot give them a chance. I said it before, I'll say it again; you require your children to look both ways before crossing a street every time, and with good reason. The same vigilance is required with computer use. Every time.

The Internet contains more good than bad. The problem is that the bad does a good job of coming to you. Pornography is big business. It will not go away. A few simple steps can make the difference.

Chapter 3

Search Engines

Harry S. Dent, Jr. in his book, *The Roaring 2000's: Building the Wealth and Lifestyle You Desire In the Greatest Boom In History,* goes to great length to inform the reader that the computer revolution is not only one of the fastest cultural changes in history, but that the computer, and more precisely, the Internet, is the most revolutionary since the invention of the printing press. Harry Dent explains that the product cycle curve for the Internet is the same as for other products, but that the time frame is much shorter. In virtually no time at all, practically all the United States will be Internet connected. Europe and parts of Asia are not far behind. I recommend that you get a copy of Harry Dent's book. You can contact the H.S. Dent Foundation at 1-800-371-9119 or visit their Web Site at *www.hsdent.com.* The work Harry Dent does on demographics is incredible.

The Internet will offer a new way of living for all of us. The microwave, camcorder, VCR, and computer all really came into their own in the last twenty years. Now the Internet is not just a toy for rich kids, but a tool for business, a shopping outlet, library, information center, a communications forum, and more. The possibilities are endless.

When the printing press came into its own in the late 1400's it changed the way the world lived. Books prior to the printing press were hand copied and could contain errors with each copy. With the printing press thousands of copies could be printed in no time at all. Enough books were now printed for the general population of Europe to learn to read and afford to own books. Books were no longer for the rich or privileged.

Look what happened after the printing press. A remarkably free flow of information ensued to the masses and religion experienced a Reformation. The Reformation of the Christian church was attempted for centuries with little result. The ability to get the word out, anonymously in some cases to protect the author's life, allowed the general public to make their own decision. In the past, if one monk wanted to institute some reform he was silenced and things continued as before.

Books became plentiful. Great libraries were built and individuals could afford a library of their own. With this vast amount of information it became difficult to find what was needed quickly. So libraries started to catalog books by the name of the author, title, and subject. Large books would have an index to easily find material among the pages.

And so, books changed the world and continue to do so. With books came the cataloging system and indexes.

The Internet is no different. In the beginning when few people used the Internet and information was scarce there was little need for search engines. However, Internet gophers existed, but they were difficult for the general public to use and were not all-inclusive.

With the search engines available today, like Yahoo, InfoSeek, HotBot, and Dogpile, it is easier to find what you need. All these search engines attempt to be all-inclusive, but are not. Some, like Yahoo and Dogpile, get close. Dogpile is unique in that they search other search engines.

With that said, it is time to have a short discussion on search engines and then parental controls.

The Major Search Engines

There are several search engines available and more breaking into the market all the time. Most search engines are free to use and get their revenue from advertising.

A few of the major search engines available include, Excite, Bigbook, Looksmart, HotBot, InfoSeek, Who Where, Yahoo, and Lycos. Yahoo is the biggest and most profitable at the time I am writing this. However, the search engine business is highly competitive. Each search engine has its strengths and weaknesses. You should experiment with several to find which one works best for you.

As shown in the previous chapter, innocent searches can lead to interesting and unexpected results. The good news is that many major search engines (like Yahoo) offer short cuts to areas of high interest on Internet without doing a search. Topics include news, culture, science, education, government, business, entertainment, regional, arts, and more.

Many search engines now offer a nicely packaged format. America Online is not the only way to get an easy to use layout. The search engines use the entire Internet, thereby, frequently offering a larger universe to travel in. Best of all, these Internet links are very family oriented. Generally, pornographic and indecent Websites are filtered out.

Games are available through AOL and the Internet. Search engines offer connection to a wide variety of virtual online games. You can play one-on-one, a little solitaire by yourself, or a massive space conquest game with hundreds of people around the country. Search engines like Yahoo offer easy access to safe and enjoyable, family oriented fun.

Dogpile

Dogpile.com is a unique search engine that I feel needs a separate explanation.

Dogpile does offer some quick links to business news, weather, stock quotes, and so forth. But Dogpile.com is best used as a huge scoop of several search engines.

When you enter a search on Dogpile.com, here is what you get. The Dogpile search engine will go to several other search engines and give you their top ten listings. You review each search engine before moving on to the next. This gives you a much wider grab on the subject you are interested in.

Dogpile will search Websites plus Usenet (newsgroups), FTP, several business and general news services.

You can set several features on Dogpile so you get the information you want. You can request a search of just the Web or Usenet and then stop or other combinations. You don't waste time either as you can put a time limit on how long it takes to retrieve the requested information; twenty seconds is the default time. Just click the 'Fetch' button.

Dogpile is free to users and is supported by advertising revenue.

America Online

America Online bought a search engine called NetFind several years ago. This not a bad search engine, but it is limited in scope. Personally, I use Yahoo and Dogpile with rare exception.

AOL has a vast Internet connection. From any Internet provider you can access *aol.com* and other Web Sites run by AOL. All this is in addition to the material available on the regular AOL service.

Keep in mind that the material retrieved from NetFind does not always pass the editorial approval of America Online. Remember that NetFind is a search engine. America Online controls the content on their computers but not what comes in from the Internet at large.

Parental Controls

Leaving your child alone with an Internet connected computer, even with parental controls, is a recipe for disaster. In many cases, once a child reaches twelve or so, they are able to by-pass parental controls faster than you can install them.

The idea of parental controls is offensive. They restrict what information can be seen, both good and bad. Adults, in my opinion, should never be restricted in what they see. Information is what we need to make quality decisions, without it we make mistakes. Parental controls, unfortunately, are a necessary evil parents need to consider to protect their children.

Parental controls work by restricting certain words. This can weed out virtually all pornographic and indecent material. It can also block out legitimate and informative Websites as well. These so-called "filters" will not allow any Website to download or list from a search engine that has the offending word.

Several parental control programs are available over the counter. Discussing them here is beyond the scope of this book. If you would like an in-depth book on this subject I recommend *A Practical Guide to Internet Filters* by Karen Schneider.

Over the counter parental control programs are available for Netscape and Microsoft browsers. One comment I do want to make is that if you are going to get a parental control type of program, get one that allows you to choose which words are excluded. This gives you greater control.

Another problem with restricting your child's access to the Internet is how you handle each child in your home. You can set up sub-accounts for each child on AOL and with other Internet providers as well. However, the more children you have the easier it will be for the younger ones to get access to an older child's password and access. There are some serious issues related to this. I will go deeper into this in chapter eight, 12 Internet Tips to Protect Your Family.

America Online has over 12 million members as I write this and they seem to add large numbers more each month. AOL also appears to be the Internet access of choice for families. Therefore, I will talk a little about AOL's parental controls.

No parental control program is perfect, but I do like the way AOL has set their system up. They have four levels to their controls: Kids Only (age twelve and under), Young Teen (age 13-15), Mature Teen (age 16-17), and Adult. You can also customize certain features like Chat Rooms, e-mail, newsgroups, file downloads, and the Web. I really like the flexibility parents are afforded at AOL.

I do disagree with the age recommendations they have for the Kids Only category. America Online set up for Kids Only allows for very little except a few games and such. Everything is gutted to virtual nonexistence. The Kids Only category will not allow your child to send or receive Instant Messages which is good. Nor will they be allowed in member-created Chat Rooms; children should not be in Chat Rooms anyway for reasons listed in the last chapter. They will be denied access to premium services, which is ok, I guess. And your child will only be allowed to receive and send text-only e-mail. This is very good; no pictures can be attached.

The restrictions don't allow your child to do much. In the Kids Only category your child has only very limited Internet access and AOL's Kids Only channel. Once your child reaches age eight or ten this category may be too restrictive. An alternative is to allow Young Teen or Mature Teen access with some adjustments to the Custom Controls.

The Young Teens category is for ages thirteen to fifteen. In this category your child will have access to some general Chat Rooms, always a bad idea. More Internet access is allowed and newsgroups that do not attach files are allowed.

Mature Teens are allowed even greater access, but similar to Young Teens. The Adult category has no restrictions.

The best approach may be to select the Young Teen or Mature Teen category and then set the Custom Controls to fit your child's maturity level.

Chapter 4

What, Where, Why: How To Find Pornography Hidden In Your Computer

Imagine you have yourself a nice little business going with a handful of employees. Imagine that each of these employees have their own computer at their desk and that your computers are connected through a network.

Business is going along just fine until one day when you overhear two employees talking about pornographic material they exchange over the Internet.

Fearing a sexual harassment lawsuit if a female employee were to be approached with indecent photography you attempt to check your computer for any unwanted files. You sit down at your computer to begin a system wide check of your network when you realize you have no idea where to begin.

When you get home that evening you notice your sixteen-year-old son and his good friend from school surfing the Internet. As you walk into the room they hush-up as your son enters a few quick commands on the keyboard. You wonder: Could my son be involved with some of the pornography we hear so much about on the news?

You spend the night tossing and turning while you come to no firm conclusions on how to monitor Internet use at home or work.

The next day you overhear some of your son's classmates talking about some neat pictures they got over the Net. Could your son be experimenting with pornography? What if he meets a stranger online and gives out some personal information? Could your family end up being stalked?

At work you call a conference to inform all employees of company policy. The Internet is for work. Pornography of any kind downloaded to a company computer will result in immediate dismissal. Of course you have no way to regulate this. Hopefully the warning does the job.

Your situation may be different from the businessman above. However, there are some serious concerns you face that if you use a computer. Anyone with access to your computer can easily get your password and use your account for their personal activities.

How do you regulate your own computer at home? Or your account at work? If you are a manager or business owner, how do you regulate and monitor the activities of your employees or the people you are in charge of?

In this chapter I will share some simple ways you can use to take control of your computer or network. Step-by-step I will show you how to find and clean your system of unwanted files, including hidden and encrypted files.

You will not require massive computer knowledge or experience. This book is for parents that want to regulate their computer even if they have very little experience. I will go step by step for Windows 95 and DOS for people with other operating systems. I will not cover any Mac computers.

By the end of this chapter and the next you will be able to find and clean your system of any unwanted picture, movie, compressed, or encrypted files. I will also show you how to take control of your Internet account and how to detect where your children have been on the Net, including the files they viewed or downloaded.

Picture Files

Pictures can now be downloaded to your computer from newsgroups and stored on your hard drive. In the past you were required to download the picture in code. Then you needed a special decoder (UUDECODE) to decode the file into a picture before it could be viewed. This is not always true anymore.

Today, with newer computers, the decoder is built in. In other words, you can view the picture as your computer receives it without downloading it to your hard drive. However, it may still be in a temporary Disk Cache file on your hard drive. If you wish to keep the picture you just save it to disk. You will still need to decode the picture you save to disk before you can view it.

Some pictures that are not supported by your Internet access software may come across your screen as junk letters and will also need to be downloaded and decoded before the picture can be viewed.

If you see junk letters instead of a picture, you have no idea what the picture contains. Therefore, once you download the picture and decode it you will need to decide if you wish to keep it. This is a larger task than you may think. When you download files, generally, you download large quantities so you don't have to wait for the computer. You just download several files and review them at a later date. This can be risky as files downloaded could contain a virus or unwanted photography. If you never run the program containing the virus you are probably ok. However, if you download picture files and do not review them all you could have some surprising and unwanted material that is just wasting disk space.

If you have been on the Internet for any amount of time you will need to take an inventory periodically to see what you have. This inventory process is also valuable to examine any material your children may have downloaded as well.

Picture files usually end with:

.jpg,
.gif.
or .bmp.

This is not always true, however. Other possibilities include:

.dxf
.cgm
.eps
.hpg
.pic
.pct
.drw
.pcx
.tif
.tga
.wmf
.wpg
.mst
and .shw.

There are more, but I think you get the idea. Besides, anyone can come along with another format and add to the list.

Now I am going to show you in a step-by-step process how to find picture files on your computer. Later I will show you how to find pictures your children viewed without downloading them to your hard drive. Either way, you will have a good idea on how much, if any, pictures are viewed with your computer.

I will assume that most people are using Windows 95. If you are using a different environment I will also show you how to do the same thing in DOS, the old fashioned way.

Windows 95 makes it easy to find something on your hard drive. Here are the steps to accomplish this.

Step #1. Click the Start button in the lower left-hand corner of the screen.

Step #2. Move the pointer to the Find directory and then click 'Files or Folders'.

Step #3. Under the 'Name and Location' tab put in the 'Named' box:

*.jpg, *.gif*

Virtually all picture files use these two formats.

Step #4. Under the 'Date Modified' tab check the box for files changed in the last month.

Step #5. Hit Enter.

This will give you a listing of virtually all picture files that have been downloaded or modified on your computer in the last month.

Picture files of all sorts can show up on this kind of listing. If in Step # 4 you asked the computer to show these kinds of files from all dates you would be greeted with a host of picture files used to run Windows and other programs, not pornography. By limiting your search to the last month you will only see the most current picture files.

Another quicker way to check for pictures on your system is to use the 'Advanced' tab under the 'Files and Folders' search. In the 'Of Type' selection you can click the down arrow and see a whole host of different types of searches you may wish to perform including several kinds of picture searches.

One more note: You will need to perform this search on every drive you have to make certain of your computer's contents.

If you are on an older system such as DOS or other environment you can still check the contents of your hard drive. You will need to exit to the DOS prompt to do this if you are in a Windows or other environment.

Here are the steps needed to complete your search.

Step # 1. At the DOS prompt type:

cd [Enter]

then:

*dir /p /s /o:-d *.jpg* [Enter]

This will give you a list of all files from the most recent to the most ancient on your hard drive including directories. The list of files will pause at a full page for you to review. Hit Enter again for another page until all files have been listed.

Step # 2. Do this for all drives on your system and also do a search for .gif files by entering:

*dir /p /s /o:-d *.gif* [Enter]

Your children or employees can be very good on a computer and hide files. To find hidden files use Step # 3.

Step # 3. At the DOS prompt enter:

*dir /p /s /o:-d /a:h *.jpg* [Enter]

Also enter the command above with **.gif* to check for those kinds of files.

This command will list only hidden files on a drive that meet the request, a gif or jpg file. You will need to repeat the process for each drive.

This whole process will only take a few minutes and should be performed monthly on home and office computers. With DOS you will receive the most current files first. Once you review the most current you can just pass the rest.

Movie Files

Movie files are getting more common. No longer do you need to be satisfied with a still picture when movies can be had.

Downloading movies to your computer can be very time consuming. However, movies are getting more common. They have legitimate personal and business uses, but also are used to transmit pornographic material, too. Certain newsgroups cater to movies more than others do. The *bestiality* and *pre-teen* newsgroups frequently post movies.

Movie files are listed on a computer as:

.avi
.mov or
.mpg.

The same process is used to find movie files as picture files for both Windows95 and DOS. Follow the steps listed above for Windows95. For Step # 3 the entry in the 'Name and Location' box is:

**.avi, *.mov, *.mpg*

For DOS the entry for Step # 1 would be:

*dir /p /s /o:-d *.avi* [Enter]

Repeat the process for *.mov* and *.mpg.*

To find hidden movie files in DOS is also the same as for pictures. The entry at the prompt for Step # 3 is:

*dir /p /s /o:-d /a:h *.avi* [Enter]

Repeat for *.mov* and *.mpg.*

Netscape

Netscape has an additional way to check up on where you, your children, and your employees have been online, even if they never downloaded a movie or picture. A record is usually kept nine days from when a Web Site or newsgroup was used. This means that every week or so you may wish to review the contents of this record.

If a picture has been viewed from a newsgroup, but never downloaded onto the hard drive a record of the file is still kept for several days. You will not know what the file contains, but the name can give you a good idea of the subject.

To see this record, start the Netscape browser. Remember that this only works if you use the Internet with Netscape. In the 'Location' box, type:

about:global [Enter]

A text file will appear listing each entry. If you see several *.jpg* files listed with names like, *hotbabe.jpg* you will have a good understanding what is there. You may also wish to have a talk with the user.

Others can access this personal information about where you have been. When you visit a Website this file can be shared with that Website. This will allow them to advertise to you or use the information for other purposes.

You may wish to empty this file on your own account to protect your privacy and once you reviewed the contents of an employee or your child's account. Here are the steps to empty this cache file.

For Netscape Navigator:

Step # 1. Click on 'Option'.

Step # 2. Click on 'General Preferences'.

Step # 3. Click on the 'Expire Now' button under 'Appearances'.

For Netscape Communicator:

Step # 1. Click on 'Edit'.

Step # 2. Click on 'Preferences'.

Step # 3. Click on the 'Clear History' button.

You may wish to do this from time-to-time to protect your own privacy.

Viewing Programs

If you find a picture or movie file on your computer and wish to view it there are several possibilities.

For picture files you can use Netscape to open the file and view it. Paint Shop and other similar programs are available.

To view a movie file you can open it in Windows using the 'Run' command on the 'Start' toolbar. The file should automatically open and run if your computer handles the format. QuickTime is a program frequently used to view movies on a computer.

If you discover a picture or movie on your computer of a pornographic nature you should erase it immediately. You also should confront the person responsible for putting the unwanted file on your system whether an employee or your child. The reason you should erase the file immediately rather than wait and confront the offender first is to protect yourself from personal liability. You are also well advised to consult with a competent attorney in computer matters to discuss these issues, especially if you are an employer that has employees online. Labor laws could also play into the situation.

Windows 95 Toolbar

You can review files that have been opened very recently in Windows by using the Toolbar and it is fast. This will tell you if an employee, child, or other user has been into picture or other kinds of files.

Simply click the 'Start' button in the lower left-hand corner of the screen and then click on 'Documents'. You will see a list of the ten most recently open files. If they are of a concern you can open them to review the contents.

To empty your 'Documents' folder just:

Step # 1. Click on the 'Start' button.

Step # 2. Move up the Toolbar to 'Settings' and Click.

Step # 3. Click on 'Taskbar'.

Step # 4. Click the 'Start menu Programs' tab and

Step # 5. Click on the 'Clear' button.

Now your documents file is empty.

Encryption

Files can be encrypted making it virtually impossible to view the contents without the pass-code. Currently there is an encryption program so good the Federal government cannot break it. Of course this will not be allowed. So the government has restricted the use of this program except for their own purposes.

If your children attempt to hide files this way there will be no way for you to tell the contents of the encrypted file. It is doubtful you could crack the code. And you don't have too.

There could only be a few reasons to encrypt a file: To hide an illegal or unethical file or to protect privacy. In business I can understand the privacy issue. However, your children doubtfully will have a legitimate reason to encrypt files.

You can find encrypted files by their size in some cases. The best way would be to use the 'Find' command on the Toolbar. You can use the 'Advanced' tab to set for files larger than say 250 KB.

Encryption is difficult to deal with and really beyond the scope of this book. It is doubtful that encryption would be used unless a serious crime is being committed, in which case, you have a problem best handled by the police and your attorney.

If you have sensitive business documents that you would like encrypted you can get a program called Away32 Delux. This program is really geared toward hiding pictures but could be a useful business tool as well. You can purchase Away 32 Delux at their Website:

www.away32.com

Other Types of Files

There are other types of files you should be aware of as well. We will cover *html* and *zip* files.

When you search your own computer you may wish to search for *html* and *zip* files. These are really encrypted files, but easy to decode. When you want to download a picture or movie from the Internet you will probably receive it in code. The reason for this is to shorten the file temporarily so you can download it faster. *Html* files are usually one picture and *zip* files probably contain several pictures. *Html* files are really known as *html*, but you will find them on your computer with the letters *html.*

Pictures cannot really be transmitted over the Internet. Instead, the picture is broken down into letters and symbols that each stand for a small piece of the picture. When these so-called junk letters are run through a decoder (UUDECODE) the picture is created matching the original. This is a binary code.

The reason to scan your computer for *html* files is to find any downloaded pictures not yet decoded.

Zip files contain more than one file. Here several files are crunched down in size for fast and easy transmission. To get at the contents you need to uncrunch (pkunzip) the file. This will break the file into several smaller files. This could be a program of any kind or a picture or movie.

Sometimes the files that are *zipped* are also in *html* code and require UUDECODE.

I will not go into the process to decode or unzip files. I want the focus of this book to remain the finding and removal of unwanted material from your hard drive and safe Internet practices.

Chapter 5

Cleaning Your System

Now that you have scanned your system you will want to clean these unwanted files from it. You also have some serious decisions to make.

If your child has downloaded pornographic material you should erase it immediately. I also recommend that you have a serious discussion with all your children, regardless of age, on the dangers and risks involved in the Internet community.

If an employee is found with pornographic material you need to talk with your legal council immediately on the labor, computer, and decency laws in your area. It is possible that an employer could be responsible for indecent material that is placed on their computer even if done so by an employee. If you are a manager you should talk to your supervisor or the company legal contact.

Deleting unwanted files can be done several ways. I will cover both Windows and DOS again.

Let's start with Windows.

Step # 1. Click the 'Start' button in the lower left-hand corner of the screen.

Step # 2. Move up the Toolbar to 'Programs' and click it.

Step # 3. Find 'Windows Explorer' from the list that pops up and select it (Click it).

Step # 4. There are several directories and files listed now. You will need to find the offending file in the directory it is located in. Follow the procedures in chapter 4 to find the file. Make note of the location (the directory) of the file. Using this information you will need to highlight the offending file in Windows Explorer. Double-click to open folders and single-click to highlight a file.

Step # 5. Once you have highlighted the offending file open the 'File tab on the top right-hand corner of the screen and choose delete. You will be asked if want the listed file sent to the recycling bin. Click 'OK'.

That is all there is to it. Repeat the steps above for each file. If a multitude of files exist in one directory you can remove the entire directory.

If you are using an older system you can also remove files in DOS. First you will need to exit to the DOS prompt.

Following the steps outlined in the previous chapter you will need to make a note of where the offending files are.

The process to remove files in DOS are:

Step 1. Move to the directory where the unwanted file resides. For example:

c*d/gifjpg* [Enter]

Step 2. To remove just one file enter:

del [name of offending file][Enter]

Example:

del sexrus.jpg [Enter]

To remove all *jpg* or all *gif* files you can use an asterisk. An example:

*del *.jpg* [Enter]

To remove an entire directory and subdirectories use this command at the c:\ prompt:

deltree/ [Directory name] [Enter]

The process is relatively simple to remove files. Once a directory is removed it is not totally gone. It can be undeleted.

If you delete a file you really need you can sometimes get it back. However, this is not a guarantee so it is best to use caution when deleting file or directories.

To undelete a file in Windows 95:

Step # 1. Click on the 'Recycle Bin' icon.

Step # 2. Highlight the file you want back.

Step # 3. Click 'File' on the Toolbar.

Step # 4. Click 'Restore' from your options.

More than likely you will want an offending file gone for good. If your Recycling Bin is full of unwanted files, pictures, and/or movies you can erase them for good by:

Step # 1. Click the 'Recycling Bin' icon.

Step # 2. Click 'File' from the Toolbar.

Step # 3. Choose 'Empty recycling Bin'.

All files in the Recycling Bin are now permanently gone. It is possible to get them back in rare instances, but we will not cover that here.

During the process of deleting files you may run across a file that refuses to be deleted. This is not a problem with your computer, a virus, or a bug. All this means is that someone added an attribute to the file.

A file that is hidden has an attribute added to it. Usually you will have to unhide a file to delete it, at least easily. A file that will not delete that is not hidden probably is set up as read-only. I will show you how to solve this problem easily in DOS.

We will tackle read-only files first.

Step # 1. Go to the DOS prompt and to the directory where the unwanted file resides.

Step # 2. Enter this command:

attrib –r [File name][Enter]

Step # 3. Follow the procedures listed earlier in this chapter to delete the file.

If you have a large number of files to delete in a single directory that are read-only the command would be:

attrib –r *.* [Enter]

Then delete all offending files.

If you have hidden files to delete they are probably read-only as well. So I will show you the process to kill two birds with one stone.

Step # 1. Go to the DOS prompt and the directory where the hidden files reside.

Step # 2. Enter this command:

attrib –r-h [File name][Enter]

Step # 3. Follow the steps listed earlier in this chapter to delete the unwanted files.

For multiple files you can also use the command:

attrib –r-h *.* [Enter]

It may take a little getting used. If you are required to clean your system often you will get the hang of it. If you are new at this or clean your system infrequently just follow the handy step-by-step process outlined above.

You can use the Windows Toolbar to keep track of any activity on your computer system. Unwanted files will show up immediately.

What If Your Child Has Given Out Personal Information And Is Now Being Stalked Online?

If you need this chapter it is because you actually found pornographic or other unwanted files on your computer. Your child in acquiring these files may have given personal information intentionally thinking nothing of it or unintentionally. Either way you may have a problem.

A determined individual with very little information can find out a lot about you. Carole A. Lane, the author of *Naked In Cyberspace: How to Find Personal Information Online*, has stated that starting with just your name and address she could learn the name and ages of your spouse and children, how you make a living, the kind of car you drive, the value of your home and the taxes on it in a few hours.

There are people that do just that sort of thing for a living. There are some people that do it for fun and not all do it legally. A lot more about you could be determined illegally as well. It is all online.

The risk that your child runs by frequenting dark areas of the Internet is not just personal involvement, but the passing of information unaware. The next chapter on *cookies* will cover this in greater depth.

Once your child has been marked by pedophiles as a target your child is in grave danger. This can happen faster than you think.

While in the process of researching this book I recorded four Chat Room conversations that are in Appendix Two. To do this I just entered the Chat Room and turned on the recorder. I said nothing at all.

When you enter a Chat Room you are listed as attending. Your e-mail address is listed, but not your real name unless you set it up in a profile.

I picked the Chat Rooms at random and recorded for about a half an hour. I walked away from my computer, talked to my assistant and took a break. When I got back I had a little more than I wanted. I received thirty-eight e-mail messages, all pornographic offers. More came in over the next weeks. I also received an Instant Message offering a good time. Just click here, they said, and I could see some good pics. I did not take them up on their offer.

Every offer sent to me was pornographic. All wanted my money too. They wanted me to go to a 'free' Web Site to see some remarkable pictures. In reality they are not free. They show you a front page similar to adult men's magazines and then tell you the really good stuff is inside for only so many dollars per month.

I have never entered one of these Websites. I can only imagine the kind of e-mail I would receive if I did.

If your son or daughter wander into something they should not have and find that personal information on them has been provided to pornographers, quick action is necessary.

First, let your Internet provider know the situation. Block all e-mail to your child and change his/her e-mail address.

Let your local authorities know the situation as well. If your child has downloaded pornography, talk with your legal council first to preserve your rights.

If you receive phone calls as a result of an Internet contact call the police immediately. Do not wait. If they know your phone number they also know your address and your child has become a target. If you need motivation on this issue review Appendix Three.

Your child may have done nothing wrong on the Internet and followed all the rules for safe conduct there and still get in trouble. Provide support to your children in their Internet endeavors. Never take chances. The high road is caution.

Chapter 6

Cookies:
These Are Not The Kind Your Mother Makes

To make the Internet more convenient certain features were added. You may have noticed that while online you can scroll back to a Website you previously used. Your computer keeps a record of where you have been and gives you an easy shortcut back. We have discussed how some of this is saved in your computer and I also showed you how to delete this information.

Computers can share information, too. In this chapter I will outline how this is done and how to limit the sharing of this information.

When computers share information it is frequently done with a file called a 'cookie'. If you have been on the Internet you have a cookie. Your cookie will contain personal information about you and where you have been on the Internet. Privacy is a large issue here. You need to take control of your cookie.

Cookies work both ways. When you enter a Website your computer may be asked to hand over its cookie. The Website will then know where and when you have been on the Internet recently. Sometimes a Website will stash a cookie on your computer too.

Now let's find the cookies on your system. I will only list Windows 95 here.

Step # 1. Click the 'Start' button in the lower left-hand corner of your Windows screen.

Step # 2. Select 'Find' on the toolbar and choose 'Files and Folders'.

Step # 3. On the 'Name and Location' tab 'Named' box enter:

*Cookies.** [Enter]

Step # 4. A list of all cookies will appear on screen. You may also have a 'Cookies' folder under the Windows directory. Double-click any of these files and you can review the cookie file. They are in text format. Now you know who is stuffing your computer with cookies.

Do not erase or change your cookie files. They are generated files. Just review them for your own knowledge.

I will now show you the steps needed to disable or rig your cookie. Keep in mind that you may want to share your cookie from time to time. If you have your own Website or want personal information shared your cookie can help. I like to order books from *Amazon.com* and I allow them to use my cookie. We both benefit.

The easiest way to disable your cookie is to use a simple program available over the Internet from:

Luckman.com

They have an anonymous cookie program available for free. This program provides other valuable, privacy retaining, features as well. This anonymous cookie can easily be turned on and off with the simple click of your mouse.

Netscape Navigator and Netscape Communicator both offer settings to restrict your cookie as well. Microsoft browsers offer similar settings. These settings can restrict the handing out and receiving of cookies. I will provide steps for both Netscape browsers, as they are the most popular.

The steps needed for Netscape Navigator are:

Step # 1. Open the Netscape Navigator browser. On the toolbar across the top of the screen choose 'Options'.

Step # 2. Choose 'Network Preferences' from the list under 'Options'.

Step # 3. A Preferences page will come up. Click on the 'Protocols' tab.

Step # 4. Check the box 'Show an Alert Before Accepting a Cookie'.

Step # 5. Click 'OK'.

Now you are ready to surf the Internet with more control. A screen will pop up every time a Website attempts to use your cookie and you can decide to refuse or proceed.

The steps for Netscape Communicator are:

Step # 1. Open the Netscape Communicator browser. On the toolbar across the top of the screen choose 'Edit'.

Step # 2. Choose 'Preferences' from the choices provided under the 'Edit ' tab.

Step # 3. On the screen that pops up you will see a tree of files listed on the left under 'Category'. Highlight 'Advanced' on the tree toward the bottom.

Step # 4. On the right-hand side of the box showing on your screen, toward the bottom, select 'Disable cookies' and check the box 'Warn me before accepting a cookie'.

I try to be as simplistic as I can when I outline these steps. It can be frustrating when you read a book or article that tells you to just 'Clean Your Cache' but neglects to say how. Your computer may be set up slightly different. If it is just use the steps above as a starting point. Your setting choices are close.

Also, feel free to change your choices to your personal preferences. I am taking the more conservative route. You may wish to be more liberal. Adjust the settings to your personal tastes. You can always use this book to help you adjust those settings later when you feel more comfortable with a particular browser.

You may wish to review your cookie from time to time as a tool to monitor where your children have been online. I personally feel that the *about:global* command is better if you are using Netscape.

Microsoft Internet Explorer is gaining ground as an Internet browser. Therefore, below are the steps needed to protect your cookie using Microsoft Internet Explorer.

Step # 1. Start the Microsoft Internet Explorer program. Click 'View' from the Toolbar at the top of the screen.

Step # 2. Choose 'Options' from the view column.

Step # 3. Click the 'Advanced' tab.

Step # 4. Check the box for 'Warn before accepting cookies'.

Step # 5. Click the 'Apply' button.

If you wish to clean the history file on Microsoft Internet Explorer, the steps are as follows:

Step # 1. Open Microsoft Internet Explorer and click 'Go' from the toolbar across the top of the screen.

Step # 2. Click 'Open History Folder' from the choices under 'Go'.

Step # 3. On the History screen select 'Edit' from the toolbar. Click on 'Select All'. Then hit the Del key on your keyboard.

And there you have it. A simple, step-by-step guide to controlling your cookie and personal information. Every time your cookie is accessed an anonymous cookie is provided from the free program from *Luckman.com.* And, anytime a Website wishes to give you a cookie, you can either accept or refuse it. Keep in mind that some Websites want your cookie bad and will not let you in without it. But it is still your choice.

You may also be interested in knowing what your computer tells other computers about you when you visit a Website. To find out what gets handed out as you surf check out the Website:

www.helie.com/Browsercheck

Dialog

Author's Note: I beg the reader to allow me a brief sidebar. This Dialog is on topic, but not necessary to protect your children, the premise of this book. I thought you might find this of interest.

At this time I want to share a little history with you. As you may have gathered, I am fond of history and philosophy. That is why I am such a big fan of the work put out by Will Durant, especially his *Story of Civilization* series.

During the course of my research I was frequently asked why such vulgarities burst onto the scene with the Internet. The answer is that it did not suddenly appear with the Internet. History will prove this out.

Western civilization generally began with Greece. Yes, we do have an Oriental Heritage and China flowered by many measures well before Western thought. And yes, Egypt moved to great heights and withered before the Greeks learned to love wisdom. But Western thought began with the Greek city-states and traveled unbroken to our own time.

The people of Greece built a modern civilization without a guidebook. Each city had its own government and they frequently fought among themselves. However, they were the first to truly experiment with democracy and freedom and rights.

The so-called Greek Empire declined and was replaced by Rome, a once Greek outpost city. Rome lived mighty for a thousand years and then fell in defeat to the barbarian hordes from the north (it was those Germans again). After the Dark Ages a light flickered in Italy and a Reformation (with the help of the printing press) blossomed in Germany, England and parts of Eastern Europe.

If you travel to Washington DC you can see our Roman history very clearly. Our government is set up after the style first used by the Romans. Even our legal system has strong ties to ancient Rome. Criminal attorneys today still use some of the legal tactics used by Seneca, the great lawyer from the Roman glory years.

What does this have to do with this book? Quite simply, many of the things we see today have its roots in the past. Pornography, bestiality, homosexuality, and other things that concern today's parents and show up on the Internet existed for a long time and frequently got their roots from ancient man.

Homosexuality is growing on the Internet, not just child pornography, which seems to make the news most frequently. The word lesbian comes from the Greek Island of Lesbos. Here the women enjoyed *free love* among themselves. This was neither hidden nor alien to the public. This kind of living was not encouraged, but not denied either.

Young boys were a special prize. Homosexuality ran rampant during the Greek glory days. This was strongly discouraged, but not denied either. Immorality was not the reason for discouragement either; it was population control. In other words, if you need more men to fight wars you need babies first and homosexuality has some difficulty with that.

Some of the greatest minds in the past preferred young children for sexual gratification and frequently of the same sex.

The famous Greek Alcibiades boasted of the men that have loved him. Xenophon exposed his infatuation with the young boy Cleinias through Aristippus. Alcman provided girls with a compliment by calling them "female boy-friends". When Plato talked of human love, he meant homosexual love. The reasons for this lifestyle are varied and the subject of another book.

In the Roman Empire this ugly vice rose again though not as often as in Greece. In the Dark Ages the practice nearly died, but so did a great many people of poverty, the plague, and starvation. Once the light of the Renaissance began to flicker we see some of the great painters taking up the practice of homosexual love with children, though they did not claim this publicly.

History has never known a period as homosexual as that of the ancients Greeks. What lead these people to this kind of living? Fear of overpopulation may be one reason, but not the overriding reason. It would seem that a billion years of human evolution has passed the genetic code down through time that is predisposed to certain lewd acts like homosexuality, child fornication, and bestiality.

These people never ceased to exist. They may have gone into hiding or suppressed their feelings, but they never went away. For the first time since 300 BC these people have a medium to ply their trade with less chance of being exposed. The Internet allows pornography to be sent to anyone to view at their leisure and with privacy. Children can be groomed over the Internet for future abuse. Right or wrong is not the point; this is the reality of our *brave new world.*

When homosexuality and pedophilia come together they find the need for fresh victims. In the recent past it took great effort and the target group was small and localized. Today, with the Internet, your target can be virtually anywhere. You can gain the confidence of a child three states away or even in another country. Once the child trusts you (or who you pretend to be), all you need do is pick them up at a predetermined place. And the child will freely go there as a bunny and full of trust until it is too late, because they have been groomed to feel they are with a friend.

The Internet did not breed a new race of perverts! They always existed. And of course, there are the millions that are just curious. In New York City people come to watch a potential suicide jumper. Yes it is gross and disgusting if the person jumps, but the urge is to watch.

Human nature responds in certain ways. If a woman screams rape people turn away. No one wants to get involved. If someone yells fire, everyone comes to take a look for three blocks around. Therefore, we need to teach women to scream fire, not rape. They will get more help and hopefully not be violated.

I am not saying that everything on the Internet is ok because people did it two thousand years ago. What I am saying is that human nature is frequently at its worst when they feel the situation is private and safe. The computer can give that false sense of safety.

Many things on the Internet are risky for adults as well as children. Parents should exercise control, too.

Parents have a duty and responsibility to understand what their children are doing. We, as parents, cannot monitor every second of our child's life, but we can provide a framework. This framework needs to be set by parents that are armed with knowledge. Without knowledge, the framework is easily insufficient.

History tells us that these issues brought up by the Internet are not new and will not go away. The police cannot protect your family, but you can. This book is the beginning, not the end. Parents should review areas of the Internet that appear in the news. This is the only way to stay current. And then, hopefully, history will not repeat itself at your expense.

Chapter 7

Legal Issues

The Internet has given rise to more legal questions than most people could imagine. Internet laws are untried in many cases and few trust how the courts will respond.

Privacy is probably the biggest issue and challenge facing Internet commerce. Your cookie is a good example. Currently, Websites have the right to see your cookie and all the information it provides as well as stack cookies on your computer. This information can be used to market products and services to you. You may not mind the offers, but many people feel they get too many offers. If you don't want the offers, it is difficult to stop them. Of course you can control your cookie, if you know how. This book has given you the knowledge you need to control your cookie, but did you know about your cookie before reading this book? How much information about yourself have you unwittingly shared? There lays the true issue. How much privacy can you feel certain of?

This book covered many topics to control how you interact with The Internet, but is not all-inclusive. When you use the anonymous cookie available at *Luckman.com* you get other privacy features too. I did not discuss them to keep this book as user-friendly as possible; I did not want to bog you down in technical jargon.

Now that you have control of your cookie other problems arise. If you set your Netscape browser to not accept a cookie without your approval you will find yourself making that decision a lot. If you have set your browser up as listed in this book and surfed the Internet you now understand how frequently your information is passed along without your knowledge. And you either pass your private information along freely or you put up with the hassle of deciding when to allow your cookie to be used.

Your e-mail box quickly becomes stuffed with offers of sex, cable converters, hot stock tip, multi-level marketing deals, chain letters and other kinds of assorted junk when your personal information is passed out. Your Internet provider can help you eliminate some of this by rejecting mail from certain sources. However, these e-mail marketers know all the tricks to stuff your e-mail box. E-mail is cheap to send and fast. Laws are sparse in this area and difficult to enforce if they do exist. The greatest concerns include the offers sent to your children. It is best to review what your children receive by e-mail.

If you would like your name removed from several direct-mail marketing lists at once you can write:

Direct Marketing Association
Mail/Telephone Preference Service
PO Box 9008
Farmington, NY 11735

This will remove your name from several mailing lists at once. You can write:

Direct Marketing Association
Mail/Telephone Preference Service
PO Box 9014
Farmington, NY 11735

to remove your name from calling lists.

America Online also allows you to control how you get your e-mail. You can choose from no e-mail to e-mail only from other AOL users, and you can exclude e-mail from certain senders. Follow these steps to set your e-mail preferences.

Step # 1. Log on to AOL.

Step # 2. Go Keyword 'Home'.

Step # 3. Double click 'Parental Controls'.

Step # 4. Click 'Fine-tune with Custom Controls'.

Step # 5. Click 'Mail'.

Step # 6. Click the 'Mail Controls' button.

Step # 7. Choose the name of the account you wish to adjust your mail settings on.

Step # 8. Click the 'Edit' button.

Step # 9. Choose your settings from the choices supplied and then click the 'Enter' button.

Now your e-mail is set to your preferences at AOL. I recommend that young children not be allowed to receive e-mail. If your child has a friend that wants to send e-mail they can send it to you and you can review the e-mail together with your child. This should be family time anyway, not a secluding process.

Another area of serious legal concern is pornography, the premise of this book. The few laws that do exist are undefined and difficult to interpret.

Many states have laws that define child pornography as illegal. Just having possession can be a crime, but what is possession. A printed copy, or a electronic copy? Is it illegal to have a photograph of your five-year-old child playing in the bathtub or a cute family heirloom? Where does the line get drawn? Who draws it?

Recently, a woman chose to have her child enter the world on the Internet. This beautiful act of life entering the world could easily be called a perversion. Why? Well, the last time I checked, Providence did not have children enter the world fully clothed. If the child is naked and obviously under eighteen years of age, this must be child pornography. Or maybe it is politics at its best.

Society must eventually decide what is acceptable or not. I am allowed to view and possess any kind of pornography because I am writing this book. So does the news reporter and magazine editor. Freedom of the press is important. I just am not allowed to print the pictures I see because child pornography is not protected by the First Amendment.

Or is it? Several books of photographs exist that show nothing but pre-teen and early teen girls in erotic posses. You can buy these books from a local bookstore or from *Amazon.com*, the Internet's biggest online bookstore.

At my local bookstore the photography section is tight against the children's section. I am amazed at how close these books are placed.

David Hamilton probably has the greatest fame when it comes to books of naked young girls. His book *The Age of Innocents* is anything but. *The Age of Innocents* shows the progression from virginity to womanhood pictorially. Here girls are shown masturbating, kissing and laying in lesbian posses, until at last a girl is laid naked on a bed next to a naked boy to be deflowered.

Is this art? Or child pornography? That is best left to the court system, I guess. But *The Age of Innocents* was ranked by *amazon.com* as the 486th best selling book they had.

Some buyers of the book commented on *amazon.com*. One reader says, "This is the best collection of art photos ever, bar none." Some comments were not as friendly. "This book is marred only by its ending, which is concerned with the end of innocents, not the living of it. If the book stayed true to its title, then it would have merely lamented the fact that a girl's innocents does end-in many cases, before its time. Otherwise, this is a wonderful book, although not as shimmering and sweet as The Fantasies Of Girls."

Opinions wary widely. You can order a slew of books of this type over the Internet. Hamilton has several. Jock Sturges is the author of *Radiant Identities* and others.

Other questions remain as well. Are parents responsible for the actions of their children? What if the parents did not know? Ignorance is not an acceptable excuse in law. But can everyone really be expected to be an expert on the Internet? Will parents be required to know more about the Internet than their children or face prosecution? I doubt it, but in a society of politically motivated District Attorneys who can tell.

I recommend several times in these pages that a competent attorney be consulted before you dig too deep on the Internet. A problem you may encounter is how do you determine if an attorney is competent on Internet issues? Attorneys, like parents, are frequently lost when it comes to Internet experience. Many Internet issues are currently being defined. What is a parent to do?

This chapter is a direct result of research. My best source came from the Internet itself. The American Civil Liberties Union (ACLU) provided me with a wealth of information. I will share some here, but I strongly encourage you to review their Website at:

www.aclu.com

The ACLU also has a site on America Online. Keyword: aclu.

Pornographic materials have been the subject of legal suits for a long time. The ACLU Briefing Paper Number 14, available on America Online, has a wealth of information. For example: several books have been banned in the past as "obscene" and/or "immoral". Many of these books we consider classics today, but faced restrictions in the past. Books like Ernest Hemingway's *The Sun Also Rises* and Theodore Dreiser's *An American Tragedy*.

Today we do not ban books too often. Books by Hamilton are granted First Amendment protection, but the law still reads that possession of child pornography is illegal in many localities. Does this mean we can produce, print and sell the book, but the buyer is a criminal?

The ACLU Briefing Paper Number 14 also answers the question, "What protects the work of artists from government censorship?" The answer begins, "Artistic creations, whatever their medium or message, and even if their content is unpopular and of poor quality, are protected by the First and Fourteenth Amendments to the United States Constitution."

Freedom of expression is not mentioned in the First Amendment, but alluded to. In the ACLU briefing Paper Number 10 they pose the question, "Why does freedom of expression play such a critical role in our constitutional system?"

They answer, "There are four primary reasons why freedom of expression, which encompasses speech, the press, assembly and petition, is essential to a free society:

"First, freedom of expression is the foundation of self-fulfillment.... Second, freedom of expression is vital to the attainment and advancement of knowledge.... Third, freedom of expression is necessary to our system of self-government. If the American people are to be truly sovereign, the masters of their fate and of their elected government, they must be well-informed.... Fourth, freedom of expression provides a "check" against possible government corruption and excess, which seem to be permanent features of the human condition."

There is more and it is truly fascinating. I recommend that parents read these briefing papers made available from the ACLU. You may also find other links available from the ACLU valuable. Keep in mind that the ACLU is looking to protect your rights, they do not want your child to be a victim of rape, incest, pornography, or torture as is found in many newsgroups.

The laws we have today are frequently not well defined. The Communications Decency Act of 1996 was cut down in 1997 for being too vague and other reasons. An interesting study for anyone is to read the material on this. Reno vs. the ACLU is available from the ACLU Website. You can also print a copy of the Motion for Preliminary Injunction on this case too. Facts and figures are everywhere in these reports and are helpful for parents as well as thought provoking.

The debate will rage on. We, as parents, have a duty and responsibility to our children. We need to provide them a good environment that is conducive to learning and safe. That may mean that our children are exposed to indecent material.

I grew up on a farm and saw life and death at an early age. This made me wise in many ways my fellow city friends were not. Just because I saw animals give birth nearly from the moment I entered the world has not scarred me or made me a pervert. It did give me an appreciation for life and the work it takes to preserve that life.

Children will be exposed to pornography eventually. This does not mean they are scared. Once your children reach a mature level you should talk to them candidly about sex, pornography and the dark side of the Internet. They will be safer with knowledge just as you are better off knowing rather than living in ignorance.

Do I advocate showing minor children some of the vulgar and disgusting pictures on the Internet? No, but you can verbally debate with your children on the subject, especially once they reach their upper teens. Many teens are experimenting with sex by this age and need guidance from their parents. If they don't get it they will go elsewhere for answers. Either way they will know. The choice is yours.

Some will argue that I have provided the exact location of some of the worst pornography on the Internet in this book and should not have. Children may see this book and use the information to explore. I agree. But do we blindfold the parents so a few children don't find the dark side of the Internet a year sooner than they normally would have? I think not. Knowledge is power. Ignorance is not bliss. Ignorance is an accident waiting to happen. Ignorance is the next child exposed and becoming a victim. Ignorance is a fool's toolbox.

The printing press allowed people the opportunity to exercise their right to know. The Internet will be just as revolutionary. Pornography will not be the only issue the Internet struggles with. Privacy will probably be a bigger issue.

Remember that even if you do not use the Internet, the Internet can affect you. Personal information about you is readily available. Information about your family is public information. How much is good or bad? That is yet to be determined.

The important thing to remember is that you must teach your children and provide a safe environment. Disable your cookie and use parental controls. Review where your children have been online and have your children sign an agreement with you to follow certain rules on the Internet. I will provide more on this in the next chapter.

Some of our most basic freedoms are continually under attack. Several fascinating discussions exist on the Internet. The best place to start is with the ACLU. They have a nice "Year In Review" type document. They also offer good legal opinion on this difficult and ever changing medium.

Happy and safe surfing.

Chapter 8

12 Tips to Protect Your Family

Safety on the Internet is a process like any other required raising a child. You need to inform children not to talk to strangers, to look both ways before crossing the street, and to share. These are basic and fundamental truths.

Society has changed and children have not. Children are insatiably curious and always will be.

How children manage their curiosity depends on how well parents and teachers communicate with the child.

A child does not know a stovetop is hot. We as parents inform the child of this fact. As a parent we may never have touched a hot burner and therefore have no personal experience. However, we get pretty excited when our children get too close to the stove. Why? Obviously, we do not want them to get hurt.

We teach our children to share and not to hit and to talk nice. These things allow our children to function well in the real world.

Before the automobile we had no need to worry about children venturing too close to the road. Before electricity we did not put safety covers on outlets. However, once these modern conveniences surfaced a set of rules sprung up around them. In this chapter I will outline twelve safety tips for you and your children for safe and enjoyable use of the Internet.

There are several family-friendly Websites out there. One I personally enjoy is:

Smartparent.com

At *Smartparent.com* they have a list of safety tips somewhat different from mine. They also encourage you and your children to sign a pledge that they provide on safe Internet practices and post it on every computer in the house. I fully support this kind of smart and proactive parenting.

Internet Safety Tip Number One:

Surf the Internet with your children.

The Internet can and should be family time. The computer should never replace the need for friends. Many sad stories that make the news echo a familiar story: "My son/daughter had a difficult time making friends so I thought the Internet could fill the void." And then there was another victim.

The Internet is a great study tool. But adult supervision is a must. Ideally, your computer should be in a general family area of the home not in your child's room. This offers easy monitoring of your child's activities. Even still, it is a good idea to check your child's activities online using the information in this book. This is not a matter of trust. Your may find someone else is grooming your child to be his next victim. You can stop this only if you know it. Knowledge is power and safety, ignorance is not bliss, it is pain, suffering and tragedy.

Internet Safety Tip Number Two:

Use parental controls when ever possible.

I personally hate the idea of parental controls. They take the real control away from the parent and give it to the programmer.

However, I am not a fool. Young children especially need severe restrictions on their Internet activity. It is just too easy for them to stumble into a hornet's nest.

Young and less mature children require at least some parental controls. Once your child has reached an adequate level of maturity the parental controls may not be needed.

America Online has a good parental control program. Several over the counter programs are ok, but some are not.

Once your child has reached fourteen years of age or older it is possible that parental controls are not needed, but they should still be supervised.

Internet Safety Tip Number Three:

Disallow the use of Chat Rooms without supervision.

As I have said before, I am not a fan of Chat Rooms. It is far to easy for a stalker or pedophile to ply his trade with little chance of being caught. If a pedophile gets caught it is usually when they try to contact the child in the real world.

Young children should not be allowed the use of any Chat Room in my opinion. Once your children reach an appropriate level of maturity they may be allowed to venture into Chat Rooms, but only with supervision.

Internet Safety Tip Number Four:

Never use a profile.

America Online and some Internet providers offer the ability to set up a profile on you. This allows you to tell a little something about yourself in a public forum, like getting to know your neighbors.

This information can be accessed by anyone at anytime without your knowledge. This would be like putting a huge ad in the newspaper providing everyone with a tidbit of personal information on you. This is something most people would feel uncomfortable doing. But the computer offers that false feeling of safety because you are in the comfort of your own home.

With a small amount of information a simple search can reveal a great deal about you. It is better to be completely anonymous online. That way you can be yourself and no one will know who you are, where you live, your lifestyle, hobbies, who your spouse is, how many children you have and their ages, and many other things.

Internet Safety Tip Number Five:

Never give personal information out over the Internet.

This is all too easy in Chat Rooms. That is why I strongly recommend that children be kept away from these areas. Profiles are personal information and also something to be avoided.

An innocent conversation can lead to the dissemination of minor personal information that an Internet search could turn into a mountain of information.

If you or your children are ever approached and asked for personal information online you should turn the matter over to local authorities. You should record the conversation, if possible, too.

Internet Safety Tip Number Six:

Don't talk to strangers—just like in real life.

There are some simple rules we all require our children to follow. We tell our children to say "no" to drugs, to look both ways before crossing the street, pick up after yourself, talk respectfully, and don't talk to strangers. Not talking to strangers has taken on a whole new meaning with the Internet.

You can never be certain who is on the other end when talking with someone on the Internet. Ghosts (people pretending to be someone they are not) are everywhere. Talking to strangers can lead to divulging personal information inadvertently.

Finding new friends online is ok if there is adult supervision or if your children are talking with a family member or friend from school.

Caution is always the best course.

Internet Safety Tip Number Seven:

Monitor e-mail your child receives.

I know this can be an unpopular thing to do and uncomfortable for the parent. However, young children should have their mail opened in the presence of a parent or guardian. As your child matures you can allow more freedom as long as your child follows the rules.

America Online parental controls allow settings that disallow e-mail or do not allow attached files. Attached files could include a virus or pornographic material.

Internet Safety Tip Number Eight:

Allow children to use newsgroups only with adult supervision.

The very nature of newsgroups offers too many opportunities for less than noble people. Therefore, children should not be allowed to use newsgroups without adult guidance until they have reached a sufficient maturity level the parents decide on.

Once your children have matured enough to use newsgroups on their own it is still a good idea to passively monitor these activities using the *about:global* command or checking your computers cookie.

Use the simple step by step suggestions offered in this book. A few minutes per month can make world of difference.

Internet Safety Tip Number Nine:

Check your cookie monthly.

It is simple and easy to check your cookie. Doing so on a regular basis gives you a firm idea on who is stuffing your computer with information that can be accessed by others.

Also, be sure to adjust your browser settings as outlined in this book to control your cookie. A few minutes spent now can save you hours later with less e-mail. It is also a good idea to protect your privacy. Besides, who wants "big brother" looking over your shoulder every step you take?

Internet Safety Tip Number Ten:

Regulate how much time your children spend online.

The computer is a great tool, but is not a good substitute for friends. Games and schoolwork can be pleasurable and a diversion with the Internet. However, excessive Internet use can lead to social problems.

Excessive Internet use could indicate time spent in newsgroups or Chat Rooms, all of which require large amounts of time online, possibly with strangers.

A good way to use the Internet is planning. Certain times of day can be available for computer and Internet use. Schoolwork time could be partially devoted to Internet research. An hour each day could be set aside to play games on the Internet or look up fun things to do. A few additional hours could be set aside each week for family time using the Internet. The parents need to set rules about Internet use and the rules should be firm.

Internet safety Tip Number Eleven:

Protect your password.

Your password protects you from unwanted and illegal use of your account. America Online will never ask you for your password, virtually no online service will. Rather than give out my password I would open a new account, canceling the old one.

If you are asked to divulge your password immediately turn this information over to your Internet provider.

If you notice unusual activity in your account inform your Internet provider quickly. There are programs that snatch your password as you log in. They are harmless viruses except that they steal your password and allow full access to your account and all private information contained there.

Some Internet browsers will respond erratically if they have been breached. If something looks out of place let your provider know.

On America Online you can check your usage under the Keyword: billing. It might be a good idea to do this monthly as well.

Internet Safety Tip Number Twelve:

Impress upon your children to never meet someone in real life they meet online without a parent.

Horror stories fill the news all too often of children and young adults that meet someone in the real world they first met online. I recommend that children never do this unless a parent actually accompanies them.

I even encourage parents not to do this. You have no idea who is really on the other end. The only exception could be if you uncovered a lost family member or old school buddy. This makes sense since it is easier to verify who this person is. If you do decide to meet a stranger a voice phone call to get to know each other first may be a good way to begin.

Final Note:

These are the twelve tips to consider. There are more that others feel are more important. These here I rank as high priority. Check out *Smartparent.com* for more information and additional safety tips.

I also like the idea of a short and simple pledge that children sign and keep by the computer. This is an agreement between the parent and child. Keeping the pledge in front of the child while they are on the Internet will keep them aware and focused on the rules.

Finally, get to know the friends your child has online just as you would friends from school. This can help you determine if your child is running with the right crowd.

The next page has a sample pledge. You may photocopy the next page and fill in the blanks where necessary. Then keep it on the computer.

Pledge

I,__________________, pledge to follow the rules my parents have given me on using the Internet.

I will:

-Never talk to strangers online

-Never give out personal information online including my password

-Only use the computer during the times my parents allow

-Never enter a Chat Room or Newsgroup without my parent's permission

-Never send my picture over the Internet

-Ask my parent's any questions I have about what I have seen online

-Tell my parent's immediately if someone asks for personal information, asks for my password, sends me a picture, or anything that make me uncomfortable online

-Never meet anyone in the real world I have met online without a parent present

____

(signed by child)

I, ____________________, promise to spend time with ______________________ online and take an interest in what __________________likes to surf online.

____

(signed by parent)

Chapter 9

Play Time and Easter Eggs

So far I have probably scared the life out of every parent. The focus on the negative side of the Internet may leave some thinking the Internet should be banned. Even after I have given you these simple and effective solutions you may still be reluctant to let your children within a hundred yards of the computer.

It really is not that bad. The Internet is mostly good. If a child drowns in a pool do you keep every child from all water forever and always? No. That would not be reasonable.

I want to share with you the little trick I played on you. This whole book has been structured the way a quality advertisement is. First I set the hook with some pain, and then I give you relief with a solution.

This is not unlike a good telephone company ad on TV where a mom is ready to leave for work and telling the kids to hurry up. Then one of the children complains she wants to go to the beach.

"I have an appointment with a very important client," the mother states.

"When can I be a client?" the youngest daughter asks.

Mom feels instant guilt and pain. Emotions race through mom's mind. If only there were a way. Then mom gets sight of the digital phone. She can do the meeting at the beach with the digital phone!

"Anyone not ready in five minutes stays home." Mom is a hero as the kids jump for joy.

Then the scene goes to the beach. The phone rings and the youngest daughter jumps up saying, "Hey everybody, it's time for a meeting."

First the pain is introduced. Then the solution that brings pleasure is given. A very powerful and motivating way to gets action, results, and sales.

I want you motivated. That is the only way you will take the action necessary to provide a safe environment for your children on the Internet.

The Internet can be a lot of fun, too. That is why I am including this short chapter on some fun and really interesting things I play with on the Internet.

This is just a starting point. There are plenty of other enjoyable and safe projects to explore on the net. I hope you and your family get a tickle out of the two I am listing here.

The first fun thing that parents may enjoy is variety. I have found a couple places on the Internet where you can actually experience commercial free radio with over a hundred varieties of music. Maybe you like the Blues or Contemporary Rock or Jazz. It does not matter. You can enjoy virtually any kind of music you want for free and without commercials. Your computer can swing up a good tune all the while you surf the rest of the Web. The Websites I use for this are:

www.spinner.com and

www.broadcast.com

Enjoy the tunes.

While you are listening to some wild tunes (did you decide to listen to some African tunes?) you can still surf the Net. I would recommend:

www.eeggs.com

This Website offers a listing of several Easter Eggs. An Easter Egg is a hidden program within a program that is interesting or fun. For example: Hidden inside Microsoft Excel 97 is a neat little program that lets you fly around and see something interesting. To get there just follow the steps listed here.

Step # 1. Open Excel 97 to a new worksheet and Press F5.

Step # 2. In the box that pops up type X97:L97 [Enter]

Step # 3. Hit the [Tab] key.

Step # 4. Press and hold the [Control and Shift] key.

Step # 5. While holding the Control and Shift key, click your mouse on the [Chart Wizard] in the toolbar at the top of the screen. It normally is toward the right side of the toolbar.

Step # 6. If you did this correctly you will be on a blue planet. You can use your mouse to fly around. There is a little surprise in there too.

Step # 7. To leave this virtual world just hit [Escape].

And there you go. You have your first Easter Egg. *Eeggs.com* has a pile of additional goodies. So the next time you want some nice clean fun and don't feel like a computer game try a few Easter Eggs. You can use the search engines to find more Websites that share these little nuggets.

I will share one more Easter Egg before I log off. This one requires the Netscape browser.

Step # 1. In the location line type *about:chouck.*

Step # 2. Click "The Swirl Society of Netscape" button at the bottom of the screen.

Step # 3. Look around the Website. A little strange, are they not? And you wonder why parents are worried about their children on the computer. Now you know what computer programmers do on their time off. Concerning.

Well, I hope you had fun. I certainly did. Maybe we will meet on the Web. In any case, have fun, play it safe, and most of all, use common sense.

Thank you for your time and for buying my book. The Pleasure has been mine.

Appendix One

This appendix lists all the newsgroups that advertise pornographic picture content at the time of this writing. This list is not comprehensive as newsgroups continually evolve. New newsgroups are added periodically.

This appendix is not intended as a search guide, however, it could be used for such purposes. Rather, my intent is to illustrate how pervasive pornography is in newsgroups, as well as how horrendous the topics. Topics such as *rape* have no redeeming value. How could a newsgroup that encourages someone to film or photograph their rape victim while being raped for inclusion in a newsgroup serve any purpose?

Hopefully, as a parent you can see the seriousness of preventing even casual contact with these newsgroups by your children. You may wish to review the content for your own knowledge, but be forewarned, I only explained what is found in these newsgroups, I did not provide examples of the types of pictures found for a reason. As always, before you intentionally enter the dark side of the Net, consult with your attorney regarding the regulations and laws in your area.

So here are the newsgroups in question. Some may seem tame, some will cause you concern. Talk with your children about the Internet and newsgroups. It is the best way to avoid problems before they begin.

The newsgroups listed below all begin with:

alt.binaries.pictures.erotica

and are followed by each of the separate listings below.

admiralrag
age.13-17
als
amateur
amateur.d
amateur.facials
amateur.male
amateur-action.gifs
ani
animal
animals
anime
anna
art.pin-up
asian
asian.male
asian-indian
australians.dropbears
autos
babies
balls
barefoot
bears

bears.moderated
bestiality
bestiality.hamster.duct-tape
bestiality.hamster.duct-tape.d
betharnold
big-folks
biker-chicks
black
black.females
black.male
black.male.feet
blonds
bobhouston
bondage
bondage.male
bondage.moderated
boys
breast
breasts
breasts.natural
breasts.saggy
breasts.small
brunette
butts
cancel
cartoons
cartoons.moderated
centerfolds
cheerleaders
child
child.female
child.male
children

close-up
commercial-websites
commercial-websites.discussion
creampie
cypher
d
d.moderated
dark-fantasy
dbg
dean-stark
denise-lester
disney
early-teens
early-teens.hardcore
earty-teens
emptynest
ex-erols
exhibitionism
exhibitionism.public
facials
female
female.anal
female.bodybuilder
female.cosmetic
female.genitalia.large
female.toys
female-ejaculation
fetish
fetish.armpits
fetish.barbie
fetish.diapers
fetish.feet
fetish.female.socks

fetish.hair
fetish.latex
fetish.leather
fetish.neck
filipinas
firesign
fisting
freckles
fuck.betharnold
furry
g-string
garters-and-heels
gaymen
gaymen.moderated
gaymen.twinks
girlfriends
gothis
groupsex
gwar
gymnast-girls
gymnasts-girls
gynecologist
hanson
hermaphrodites
high-heels
high-school
horneyrob
horneyrob.d
hubbs-is-a-dick
indian-asian
interracial
istar-diapers
jap.schoolgirl

jay.t.carrigan.wife
karl-malden.nose
kerri-maskol
kibology.PGP
kmart
koo-sisters
kwakivtl
lame
latina
latino
legs
lesbian
lesbians
lesbians.french-kiss
ll-series
lolita
male
male.anal
male.bodybuilder
male.bodybuilder.moderated
male.burly
male.chubby
male.oral
male.oral.cumshots
male.tattoos
marcusvilliers
Mardi-gras
mf-action
midgets
moderated
nativeamerican
nipples.large
nose

olderman
oral
oriental
orientals
panties
party-girls
partygirls
pirate.mag
plushies
pornstar
pornstar.jenna-jameson
pornstars
pornstars.ariana
pornstars.janine.moderated
pre-teen
pre-teens
pregnant
puffies
pw-series
rape
redheads
safetyvest
scanmaster
scheherazade
schoolgirls
shave
spam
spanking
spanking.damian-j-anderson
spanking.schoolgirl
spanking.teen
spatch
sprintlink

stacey-owen
stockingsex
tasteless
teen
teen.d
teen.fe
teen.female
teen.female.fuck
teen.female.masterbastion
teen.female.masturbation
teen.female.nonude
teen.female.orgasm
teen.fuck
teen.male
teen.masturbation
teens
teensex
terry.agar
thigh-highs
torture
transvestites
uncut
uniform
uniform.male.moderated
unix
upskirt
urine
vintage
violence
voyeurism
voyeurism.hidden-camera
wetspot
young

zig.and.zag

As you can see, nearly any perverted taste can be satisfied. Our number one job as parents is to make sure our children are not in the picture.

Many of these newsgroups do not contain many postings. Some, like *rape,* contain around 500. *Early-teen* and *pre-teen* carry around 4,000 on average. This can give you some idea of how pervasive this is.

Appendix Two

Below are some real examples I recorded off America Online Chat Rooms. Most Chat Rooms end up the same way, in an attempt to get personal information from all the attendees, age and sex checks, and offers of pornographic pictures.

It is not hard to argue that children are best served by staying away from Chat Rooms. The risks are too great. As a parent you may not wish to participate in a Chat Room, so I included several examples below. Remember that these are real life, not mock-up examples I created. Nothing has been changed. This is how they really appeared on my computer screen.

Example Number One

From the AOL Chat Room: Romance--The Flirt's Nook

Angie93778: hey guys what's up?
Playn4PGA: not alot, Angie what you up too
BUDICE32: so how lod are you fogline?
Built41: what up angie
BUDICE32: old
Fogline1: 31
BUDICE32: sorry
Angie93778: jus chillin
Fogline1: and you
BUDICE32: cool your still young
BUDICE32: 22/f
Fogline1: YES!!!!!!!!!!!!!!!!!!!!!!!!!!!
Playn4PGA: any ladies wanna chat?
Angie93778: age/sex check
BUDICE32: so do you have any kids fogline
Fogline1: M/#!
Fogline1: #!31
Angie93778: 17/f
Playn4PGA: 28/m
Fogline1: 2
BUDICE32: i have a son 7 months old
Fogline1: I raise them by myself
BUDICE32: are you married
Yazstonken: HELLOOOOOOOOOOO ROOM!!!!!!!!!!!!!
Fogline1: no she ran off with a sailor
Fogline1: in 92
BUDICE32: oh i guess your not married
Angie93778: hey6 YAZ
Barrett987: hello room
Fogline1: now she regrets it but oh well!!!!!!!!!!!!!!!!!!!!!!!!!!
Yazstonken: wsup angie?
Angie93778: being bored u?
Yazstonken: same here
Yazstonken: age?
Fogline1: have a nice day got to go to work
Andimat: hello?

GRVLTRVL: hello all 24/m/pic here
AHHDBALL: Helll Oh Chatpeople whats glowi on in here?
MARLMAN1: hello ladies any females want to private chat?
Andimat: I would love to private chat
Smurfy7932: hey whats up
AHHDBALL: Are we alive in here 2day?
Danimal476: Age/Sex ceck
JStarlit: 15/f here, hello everyone!
Danimal476: 15/m here
AHHDBALL: Hi js
Mayhemaybe: Greetings all.....29 male
JStarlit: hey!
Danimal476: oh hi Js
Smurfy7932: 16/f
MARLMAN1: only females please 32/m
JStarlit: hello Danimal!
Danimal476: HI!
AHHDBALL: Good Day Smurfy whats glowin on?
Gmanltd: hello room
Mayhemaybe: <Jumping up and down> Hello!!!!!
Teddy47361: HEY PEOPLE
Cikem78: HI
Gmanltd: anything exciting going on in here
KatieeL16: hi mayhemaybe
Teddy47361: im tired!
Smurfy7932: nuthin wuz up with you im just babysittin
Cikem78: ANy ladies here?
Teddy47361: me
Teddy47361: 13/f
Cikem78: Hullo Teddy
Cikem78: ACk 13
Teddy47361: hey
Teddy47361: cool
AHHDBALL: I,m sacrificing my roomies hamster to Rob Zombie
JStarlit: 15/f
Gmanltd: jailbait
Danimal476: 15/m
Smurfy7932: 16/f
Gmanltd: so many people but no talking
Gmanltd: why is that
Danimal476: anyone want to chat? IM me
JStarlit: what's up?
Gmanltd: the sky is up
Smurfy7932: hey what up Gman
Gmanltd: I feel old in here

JStarlit: very funny
Smurfy7932: how old are you
AHHDBALL: I dont blame you GMAN
Teddy47361: thats not the only hting thats up
Twist73468: hello 20/m
Mayhemaybe: I keep getting these damn Porno Advertisments!
Gmanltd: Age/Sex Check
AHHDBALL: but everybodies different
Teddy47361: 13/f
Twist73468: 20/m
Smurfy7932: 16/f
Mayhemaybe: 29 male and yes......I have it
Sheller3: hello room
Cikem78: ?/m
BEister629: 15/m
Gmanltd: 21/m
Sheller3: 18/m
Cikem78: <- thinking about it
Twist73468: to many guys
Gmanltd: not enough f
AHHDBALL: 25/m/genius
Angel35188: Hello all 22/f here that is as sweet as honey
Mayhemaybe: {S systemstart
BEister629: 15/m
Mayhemaybe: Hee-hee!
Gmanltd: Hello Angel
Angel35188: hello GM
Gmanltd: finally a woman of legal age
Cikem78: Hello ANgel
Angel35188: Hello CIK
Angel35188: LOL
Gmanltd: how are you today Angel
AHHDBALL: Angel
Cikem78: CAn I marry you ANgel?
Angel35188: ok i think that means we need a AGE/ SEX CHECK PLEASE
Teddy47361: ahh put my shoe on wronge
Angel35188: great thanks u
Cikem78: 20/m
Smurfy7932: no one is talking
Angel35188: yes AHH
AHHDBALL: you certainly r popular
Mayhemaybe: 29 male
Mayhemaybe: male
Gmanltd: 21/m

Angel35188:	why CIK
Mayhemaybe:	29
Mayhemaybe:	29
Mayhemaybe:	and male
Gmanltd:	fine but bored
Cikem78:	You are and ANGEL TO ME
Mayhemaybe:	Did I say I was 29 ???
Mayhemaybe:	And male??
Angel35188:	ahhhh thanks CIK
Angel35188:	LOL MAY
Smurfy7932:	16/f
Mayhemaybe:	<Silly grin>
Angel35188:	i like a man with wit
Cikem78:	DO you have a bf ?
JoxerEAD:	hello everyone
BchGrl2012:	hi room
Angel35188:	no
Cikem78:	LOL
Mayhemaybe:	<---lots-O-wit
BchGrl2012:	28/f
Cikem78:	Why not?
Gmanltd:	hello Bch
BchGrl2012:	hey gm
Angel35188:	are you intelligent too
Cikem78:	Yes I am
Mayhemaybe:	But of course my love....
Gmanltd:	How r u today Bch
Angel35188:	wow i just lucked out now didnt i
BchGrl2012:	fine, how r u?
Cikem78:	LOL
Dirtyz80:	hey any flirts want my nook
Gmanltd:	ok just a little bored though
Angel35188:	so where ya'll from
Cikem78:	CA
Smurfy7932:	hell ya dirty
Gmanltd:	a place far far away
Angel35188:	LOL
Angel35188:	which is where
BchGrl2012:	I took the day off work and now I`m baby sitting
Gmanltd:	if I told you I would have to kill you :)
Smurfy7932:	dirty age/check
Angel35188:	well todays a good day to die so tell me
Angel35188:	{S stupid3
Angel35188:	{S hvnsnt

Gmanltd: no day is a good day to die
Angel35188: hey now you dont know that
Smurfy7932: bch im baby sitting too
Gmanltd: call it a lucky guess
Mayhemaybe: {S slitwrists outta boredom
Angel35188: I mean i am an angel anydays a good day for me LOL
Gmanltd: <--- is not babysitting
Angel35188: dot do that MAY id miss you
Gmanltd: lol
SPANK DIS: one day your here and the next day you gone
Madforker: any f wanna teach me to CYBER im me
Mayhemaybe: {S band-aide
Angel35188: teach you to cyber like thats so hard
Riker678: age/sex check
Angel35188: 22/f
Gmanltd: to live is to die but it is what you do in between that counts
Angel35188: ahhh MAY let me help you
Mayhemaybe: ????<PERK>
Angel35188: thats right GM
Madforker: new to online
Angel35188: <-------putting bandaid on MAYS wrist
Gmanltd: old enough/ not yet today
Mayhemaybe: Thanks my love....I may have to run off quickly......
Mayhemaybe: Put me on Buddy list???
Angel35188: why sweetie
Prynses8: hey everyone 15/f here
Mayhemaybe: I should be on after 10 Thursday
Angel35188: hmmmmm :-(
Angel35188: i heal the wounded and they leave me
Mayhemaybe: My friend just go online...haven't spoken in 3 months!
Angel35188: what a shame
Angel35188: hmmm
Gmanltd: oh I see
Angel35188: sniff sniff
Gmanltd: this is touching
Angel35188: LOL GM
Prynses8: age/sex check
Teddy47361: I CAN STICK MY TONGUE UP MY NOSE
Gmanltd: should I play my heart bleeds for you
Mayhemaybe: I'm soo sorry love...I must fly.....

Angel35188: <-------thinkin GM is gonna get doused with a water ballon if he not nice
MBen135897: hi room
Gmanltd: I am always nice
Angel35188: good bye MAY goodbye
JoxerEAD: 18/m
Mayhemaybe: Parting is such sweet sorrow and all that.....
Mayhemaybe: I'll lokk for ya tHursday.
Angel35188: <------------throws a water ballon at GM ahahhahahahaha
Angel35188: yeah yeah
MBen135897: 20/m looking for lady
Mayhemaybe: <BAMPF>
Gmanltd: <splash>
Angel35188: hahahahahahaha
Gmanltd: I needed that
Angel35188: good glad i could oblige
Gmanltd: do it again
Gmanltd: such hostility
Angel35188: <-------throwing another water ballon at GM
AHunter738: hi

Example Number Two

From the AOL Chat Room:
Town Square—bestlilchathouse

MBarr21188: FHJKGLRHUIRQGKQ
Jiraf77: NO
BETCJIM: WANT TO CHAT?
Cmass123: will anyone chat with a 13/f model? Hey Diw
AGISLUCY: SUBZEROXKI,WANNA CHAT WITH ME/ IM 14 AND IM A BLONDE.
MBarr21188: FDSFDHGTE
SUBZEROXK1: YES I DO
Jiraf77: dus n-e-1 want my pic???
BigiE20: hello all
MBarr21188: BLONDES ARE GOOD AT ALOT OF THINGS THEY CAN JUMP AND YELL AT THE SAME TIME
Jiraf77: hyu
SUBZEROXK1: WHERE CAN I FIND YOU
AGISLUCY: CMASS 123.IM 14,AND IM A MODEL TO.WHAT AGENCY DO U GO TO?
BETCJIM: SUBZERO XK1 ARE U F/M?
AGISLUCY: SUBZEROXKI,ARE YOU TALKING TO ME?
XOiPunk: **¤÷¥÷ºº±÷¥÷(¥)ÅLíÇ£ Ï/\/ \X/Ø/\/Ð£|²›Lª/\/Ð íŠ GøÐ÷¥÷±ºº÷¥÷¤**
SUBZEROXK1: I AM A MALE
Diw1998: ANY 12-14 F
BETCJIM: HOW OLD ARE U?
Diw1998: I MEAN M
MBarr21188: YOU KEEP THINKING THAT
SUBZEROXK1: YES I AM
MBarr21188: ARE YOU SURE
AGISLUCY: COOL

VVCheer99: •¤•´¨¨\/¨¨` •¤•Smile for camera.........

VVCheer99: •¤•´¨¨\/¨¨` •¤• <CLICK>

VVCheer99: hey everyone

AGISLUCY: WANNA GO TO A PRIVATE CHAT ROOM?

Alagra6093: hel'o

BETCJIM: DIW1998 IAM 13 AND I WOULD LIKE TO CHAT

VVCheer99: anyone from pa?

Alagra6093: nope

MBarr21188: I AM

VVCheer99: where?

NorthW15: any fine bitches who wanna cyber with a hot 16/m press 69 or im me

SUBZEROXK1: WHAT DO YOU WANT TO TALK ABOUT AGISLUCY

Alagra6093: 69

NorthW15: im me

MBarr21188: L.A.

Alagra6093: anyone want to chat with 15/f?

NorthW15: yeh

AGISLUCY: NORTHW 15,ILL CYBER YOU. IM 14 AND WOULD BE HAPPY TO,JUST TAKE ME TO YOUR ROOM!!

Tweetykd: Hello everyone

Alagra6093: im me

BETCJIM: 1998 I WANT TO CHAT WITH U

AGISLUCY: WHATEVER YOU DO SUBERZOXKI

MBarr21188: I'LL CHAT WITH YOU ALAGRa

MBarr21188: 16/M

Alagra6093: 15/f

SUBZEROXK1: I BUILD THINGS WITH MY HANDS

Reiches21: AGE/SEX CHECK

Tweetykd: 15/f

Alagra6093: im me and we will chat

MBarr21188: WHERE ARE YOU FROM

Cmass123: Does anyone want to chat with a 13/f

Alagra6093: alabama you

Tweetykd: How old are you Reiches?

Reiches21: 16/m

MBarr21188: BRYAN ,TEXAS

Shlh: 17/f

SLopez7698: does anyone wanna cyberg with a 17/m

Jiraf77: 15/f

Alagra6093: my mom use to live there

Cmass123: alagra- what part of Alabama?

Alagra6093: unstville
MBarr21188: WHATS YOUR REAL NAME
BETCJIM: REICHES21 I WANT TO CHAT
Tweetykd: Where is everyone from?
Alagra6093: hunstville i mean
Jiraf77: n-e-1 wanna a pic???
Reiches21: age/sex BETCJIM
Alagra6093: alagra
AGISLUCY: SLOPEZ,I WILL
Reiches21: NY
Jiraf77: im frum LA
Jiraf77: 15/f
SLopez7698: what's up AGISLUCY
MBarr21188: MINE'S IS MAX
Tweetykd: I'm from Ohio
BETCJIM: 16/F
AGISLUCY: NOT MUCH,WANNA GO TO A PRIVATE ROOM?
Alagra6093: cool im me and we can talk
SLopez7698: yea baby
MBarr21188: WHO
SUBZEROXK1: DISCRIBE YOURSELF AGISLUCY!!!!!
AGISLUCY: CAN YOU TAKE ME THERE?
Alagra6093: what who
SUBZEROXK1: TAKE YOU WHERE?
MBarr21188: WHO DO YOU WANT TO IM YOU
Alagra6093: you
Reiches21: IF UR FROM NY GIMME A HELL YEAH
MBarr21188: OH OK
AGISLUCY: SUBEROXKI,IM SORRY,IM BLONDE 5FOOT 4 AND HAVE BLUE EYES.U/
Reiches21: HELL YEAH
SLopez7698: don't know how to get a private room
NorthW15: hey AGISLUCY go into northw15 private chat
AGISLUCY: TO A PRIVATE ROOM!!!
Emilyprez: HELLO
SUBZEROXK1: I'M 5FOOT 5INCHES BROWN HAIR + BROWN EYES
Emilyprez: WWWWWWWWWWWWWWWWWEEEEEEEEEEEEEEEEEEEEEEEEEEEEEEEEEEEEEEEEEEEEELLLLLLLLLLLLLLLLLLLLLLLLLLLLLLLLL
SLopez7698: so what's gonna happened AGISLUCY
Emilyprez: SO
Emilyprez: im gone bye

Reiches21: Reiches 3:16
AGISLUCY: I DONT KNOW,SLOPEZ,I DONT KOW HOW TO GET INTO A PRIVATE CHAT ROOM!
Alagra6093: wheres mbarr
Oceandrm88: hello people
Alagra6093: hi
SLopez7698: Ill get back 2 u in SEC. hang in there ok
Alagra6093: anyone seen mbarrr?
Oceandrm88: nope
AGISLUCY: K
Emilyprez: no
Reiches21: who is mbar
MBarr21188: i'm right here
RLong12260: good morning everyone
LP747: any women out there?
Alagra6093: some one who imed me and i lost the connetion
Emilyprez: i dont know
AGISLUCY: LP747.IM A WOMEN!!
Alagra6093: right here
MBarr21188: i i.m you but nothing happened
Oceandrm88: hey
Alagra6093: try again
Alagra6093: hey who
Oceandrm88: anyone listening
SUBZEROXK1: ANY 14/F WHO WANT TO TALK TO A 14/M ?
Cmass123: i think this is an awesome chat room!
Oceandrm88: why?
Cmass123: 13/f
Emilyprez: i like mobile
Oceandrm88: nothings going on
Reiches21: if u wanna chat with a 16/m im me
MBarr21188: alagra you im me
Cmass123: i don't know. i just do.
LP747: how old are you AGISLUCY?
Alagra6093: i dont know how to
AGISLUCY: SLOPEZ,ARE YOU BACK YET
Oceandrm88: is this room filled with a bunch of youngins or what?
AGISLUCY: IM 17
Ebradley14: HI
AGISLUCY: U?
Emilyprez: sure
Reiches21: AGE/SEX CHECK
Ebradley14: 14/F
Emilyprez: no
Cmass123: age/sex oceandrm88

AGISLUCY: 17/F
Jiraf77: 15/f
MBarr21188: ok i'll im you when you see the box click on respond
Alagra6093: mbarr you here
Oceandrm88: 18/f
Alagra6093: ok
Emilyprez: no
Oceandrm88: u cmass
Alagra6093: last time some one else im ed me and it wouldnt let me resdpond to yours
Reiches21: 16/m
SLopez7698: AGISLUCY just give me 3 MIN.
Dolphi8956: 15/m
Alagra6093: to do what
AGISLUCY: OK SLOPEZ.
Emilyprez: **bbbbbbbbbbbbbyyyyyyyyyyyyyyeeeeeeeeeeeeeeeee**
Sexy100984: who knows how to cyber
Alagra6093: i do
Dolphi8956: me
AGISLUCY: ME
Emilyprez: whats that
Dolphi8956: a 15/m here who wants to cyber HARD
LP747: what women like to talk dirty?
Dolphi8956: IM me if you do to
AGISLUCY: LP747,IIIIIDDDDOOOOO
Sexy100984: <SEXY FEMALE > In Da HoUzE
Pethousale: HELLO
Dmam411: sexy huh?
BIDDY416: hi
Sexy100984: WHO WANTS TO CYBER I GOT A NKED PIX
Pethousale: 24/F
BLueEyZ626: HI...AGE/SEX/LOCATION CHECK?
Cmass123: Age/sex sexy?
Reiches21: 16/M/NY
Megan51184: hi all
BIDDY416: 17/fs/ny
AGISLUCY: ARE YOU BACK YET SLOPEZ?IMISS YA!!!
Megan51184: any one talk
BLueEyZ626: 20/F/NY
Sexy100984: 19/GOOD LOOKING FEMALE
MHall93496: hey sexy
BLueEyZ626: WHAT PART OF NY REICHES?
Pethousale: hey megan, guess no guys want to talk

Reiches21: LONG ISLAND
Sexy100984: MHALL HEY
BLueEyZ626: OH
Megan51184: location?
Dmam411: we will talk
BLueEyZ626: I LIVE NEAR BUFFALO
BIDDY416: sexy are you a les
MHall93496: do you wanta chat a loen sexy
Reiches21: THATS PRETTY FAR AWAY FROM LONG ISLAND
Pethousale: houston, texas
Megan51184: my dad lives in buffalo
BLueEyZ626: I KNOW
AGISLUCY: HAS ANYONE SEEN SLOPEZ?
Cmass123: yes. sexy is a lesbo!
Sexy100984: NOPE I LOVE MEN
BLueEyZ626: ANY HOT GUYS WITH PICS?
BIDDY416: oh we thought you sounded like one
Megan51184: any one want to chat
Megan51184: ????????????
Megan51184: any one?
Sexy100984: NE WAYS
BIDDY416: mega?
Megan51184: ok..BYE ALL
Reiches21: IF UR FROM NY GIMME A HELL YEAH
AGISLUCY: HAS ANYONE SEEN SLOPEZ?
BIDDY416: megan are you a girl?
Megan51184: yes
BIDDY416: sure
BIDDY416: whatever
JrLejonCJ: **«•·×¤[\/é§Å P|-|¡§|-|ë®]¤×·•»**
JrLejonCJ: **«•·×¤[Status: Unloaded]¤×·•»**
JrLejonCJ: **«•·×¤[Damn, Tha <><'s Hafta Wait]¤×·•»**
Megan51184: what do u mean
BIDDY416: nevermind
Almanny: hia
Mazarine83: hi roomies
Megan51184: u don't think i am a ggirl
Clen18m: 19/m/pa
Almanny: hia how is everyone
BIDDY416: hi clen
Megan51184: BYE ALL
MHall93496: 15/f

Almanny: bye
Mazarine83: im pretty good. what about you, almanny?
JS8436: hey room
Almanny: i am good thanks
JS8436: what's up?
Almanny: age\s Maz
Cmass123: the sky
Mazarine83: 15/f
MHall93496: sexy are you on
BIDDY416: any guy want to talk to two 17 females
ECL 1982: 15/M here
BIDDY416: ?
Almanny: hey ECL
JS8436: 15/f
Wiz5331: 27/m
ECL 1982: Hi Almanny
MHall93496: 15/f
Almanny: how are you
Mazarine83: anyone like the cure?
BIDDY416: im us
K Magic28: 11/f here
Cmass123: k magic- location?
Poohbie1: hi room
Mazarine83: hey.
Almanny: anyone out there
Mazarine83: ?
JamieB08: Whats up
Mazarine83: almanny, how old are you?
Almanny: hey jamie
Almanny: 16\f
MHall93496: any one wana chat with a 15 year old girl only boys
press 15
JamieB08: Hey
Almanny: hwo are you
Almanny: how
Almanny: opps
Almanny: heheh
Bonfire476: hello
MHall93496: press 15
JamieB08: Any one from NC
Bonfire476: hello
Almanny: no one wants to press 15
Almanny: hehehehe
JamieB08: 15

Bonfire476: 15
MHall93496: thanks
Almanny: jamie age sex
BETCJIM: ANY 1 WANT TO CHAT?
ECL 1982: someone IM me
Bonfire476: age sex check
JamieB08: 13/m
Reiches21: 16/m
MHall93496: no
ECL 1982: 15/m
MHall93496: 15/f
BETCJIM: 16/F
JamieB08: How about you Almanny
Ginny21: hey yall, cute 14/f here any guys wanna chat?
Bonfire476: hi mhall
MHall93496: hi
Bonfire476: ya
ECL 1982: any girls
MHall93496: do you wanta chat
Geez420: hey whats up room
Almanny: 16\f
ECL 1982: sure
Geez420: any guys wanna chat with a 17/f
Bonfire476: <~~~hot 15/m
Ginny21: 14/f
BETCJIM: YES ECL1982I WILL CHAT
MHall93496: 15/f
Geez420: im me if u do
JamieB08: Anyone Surf
AlliGtr59: hello all
TOEDO: Hello people.
JamieB08: Anyone want to chat
K Magic28: hi alli
MHall93496: bonfire476 wana chat

Example Number Three

From the AOL Chat Room:
Town Square—Lobby

Tiamar1042:	SUP ROOM
Kill40628:	wn cude is not a known member
JumpinJ978:	16/f here
SSOTC10:	17/f
Kill40628:	11/m
Mypooh 6:	anone want to talk to a 14/f
Butrfly065:	hi 16/f
MIZTY1833:	Hello anyone want to chat w 20/f
Tiamar1042:	17/F
WNCude:	You little 11 year old Can't even punt
Kill40628:	yes i can
JumpinJ978:	any 15-19 males wanan chat im me
WNCude:	try it
Kill40628:	ill tos then
MIZTY1833:	this room sucks!!
DWill49688:	yep
WNCude:	for doing what?
BANCHEY:	age/sex/loc
DWill49688:	16/f/CA
MIZTY1833:	im signing off goodbye
Butrfly065:	16/f/ia
Prance126:	12/f
SCREAM3674:	{S IM
JumpinJ978:	16/f/mass
LadyChloee:	21/f/tx
SCREAM3674:	{S SYSTEMSTART
Kill40628:	mass
JumpinJ978:	Kill40 ahe sex

Kill40628: **...™...™...™...™...™...™**
™...™...™...™...™...™... ...™...™...™...™...™...™
™...™...™...™...™...™... ...™...™...™...™...™...™
™...™...™...™...™...™... ...™...™...™...™...™...™ PéPŠi^{2,3}
Kill40628: **...™...™...™...™...™...™**
™...™...™...™...™...™... ...™...™...™...™...™...™
™...™...™...™...™...™... ...™...™...™...™...™...™
™...™...™...™...™...™... ...™...™...™...™...™...™ PéPŠi^{2,3}
Kill40628: **...™...™...™...™...™...™**
™...™...™...™...™...™... ...™...™...™...™...™...™
™...™...™...™...™...™... ...™...™...™...™...™...™
™...™...™...™...™...™... ...™...™...™...™...™...™ PéPŠi^{2,3}
Kill40628: **...™...™...™...™...™...™**
™...™...™...™...™...™... ...™...™...™...™...™...™
™...™...™...™...™...™... ...™...™...™...™...™...™
™...™...™...™...™...™... ...™...™...™...™...™...™ PéPŠi^{2,3}
Kallie 64: hi people 15/f here anybody wanna talk
Karrey345: hey room
JumpinJ978: kill40 age sex
WNCude: hes 11
Kill40628: **• • • •···÷•••• PéPŠi** ^{2,3} **By CpRiDe And DC**
Kill40628: **• • • •···÷•••• UnLoaded By: Kill40628**
Kill40628: **• • • •···÷•••• At: 7/21/98 - 11:40:15 PM**
JumpinJ978: This Room Sux ! I'm Out Peace
Karrey345: age/sex check
Tiamar1042: 17/F
Karrey345: 13
RNolen3454: give me head
JVacca6852: 16
Kallie 64: 15/f
Butrfly065: 16/f
WNCude: Kill did you ever think that you could e-mail punt me?
Prance126: 12/f
RNolen3454: 16m
JVacca6852: 16/F
BANCHEY: 13/f
Mypooh 6: hey kill40628 where you from
RNolen3454: 16/m
CO CO7084: **(¸.·´)•[ßlún†'z**$^{1.2}$ **àntí™ ‹›ßlún†‹›**
CO CO7084: **(`·.¸)•[Status: •Loaded•**
Tiamar1042: 17/F
JVacca6852: RNolen where from
CO CO7084: **·)• PHøTøN Anti Punter Final ß¥ BLoODBaTH •(·**

CO CO7084: ·)• Now Protecting [CO CO7084] •(·
CO CO7084: ·)• Punt/Freeze Sensitivity: 666/83 •(·
BANCHEY: age/sex/loc
Butrfly065: 16/f/ia
Slash88180: hi room age/se
Slash88180: ooops
JVacca6852: 16/F/FL
CO CO7084: does n e one have n e fake i d creators????
BANCHEY: 13/f/ny
Slash88180: 15/m
Slash88180: /mich
Tiamar1042: 17/F/CT
RNolen3454: Va Beach
CO CO7084: **•÷····^v(· PêPŠi v4 Cõdêd ßý CpRiDe And DC**
•÷····^v(· Loaded ßý: "CO CO7084"
CO CO7084: **•÷····^v(· "7/21/98 - 11:42:52 AM"**
CO CO7084: **•÷····^v(· Attêntiõn Attêntiõn {S IM}**
CO CO7084: does n e one have any fake i d creators?
CO CO7084: **•÷····^v(· Attêntiõn Attêntiõn {S IM}**
Shorts2003: hey peeps
Canon 906: 1101
Canon 906: 1111
Canon 906: 1121
Nevabug: hello lovins
TamikaATL: hi everybody 15/f here
Canon 906: 1131
Canon 906: 1141
Slash88180: man your cool
Canon 906: 1621
Canon 906: 1631
Canon 906: 1641
BANCHEY: age/sex
TamikaATL: canon stop!!!!!!!!!!!!!!!!!!!!!!!!!!!!!!!!
Shorts2003: canon would u mind stopping
Canon 906: 1761
Slash88180: 15/m
Canon 906: 1771
Canon 906: sfd
TamikaATL: 15/f
Slash88180: 1781
Slash88180: oooh i beat him
SOutHParC2: i punted canons ass
Slash88180: lol
TamikaATL: how's everyone?
BANCHEY: what music does everyone listen to?

TamikaATL:	mostly r&b
Tiamar1042:	RAP AND R%B HERE
Canon 906:	2261
Canon 906:	2271
Canon 906:	2281
Canon 906:	2291
Canon 906:	2301
Canon 906:	2311
TamikaATL:	canon stop
Canon 906:	2381
Nevabug:	go away canon
Canon 906:	2511
Shorts2003:	canon STOP!!!!!!!!!!!!!!!!!!!!!!!!!!!!!!!!1
Canon 906:	2521
TamikaATL:	canon stop that damn shit
JVacca6852:	STOP Please

Example Number Four

From the AOL Chat Room: The Saloon

NATURELLLE: shhhhhhhh we all huntin wabbitts?

FelinesBat: •··÷¦[Endless3.1 **Afk** Bot - [Disabled]

R0Nl: DANG IS THIS A MORGUE OR SCREEN FREEZE??

FelinesBat: {{{{{{{{{{{{{{{{{R0NI}}}}}}}}}}}}}}}}}}}}}}}}}}

Rifle87608: THINK THE ROOM IS HAVIN A ORGY IN DA LOFT

R0Nl: {{{{{{{{{{{{{{{{{BRI}}}}}}}}}}}}}}}}}]

R0Nl: OMG

FelinesBat: AWWWWWWWWWWWWW, SHE REMEMBERED

Mikes36000: {{{{{{{{{{{{{{{{{{{{{{{{{nat}}}

R0Nl: <=-=-=-=- RUNNIN UP DA STAIRS TO DA LOFT

FelinesBat: IM S0000000000000 T0UCHED

SweetCC77: hey room, 17/f here

R0Nl: SMOOCHES BRI =)~!~

FelinesBat: CAN U T0UCH L0WER TH0??? **>=D**

FelinesBat: W00 H00 !!

R0Nl: {S RONI

SweetCC77: hey there

Mikes36000: hey

FelinesBat: WB CY

Rifle87608: You reach the limit CY?

R0Nl: <=-=--YELLIN BACK DOWN FROM DA LOFT " HEYYYYY THEY WONT LET ME IN

Cyran4life: MUCHAS GRAS

SweetCC77: anyone wanna chat with a 17/f from houston?

Cyran4life: IT MUST SUCK TO BE VIPER

NATURELLLE: WB CY. ....SOOOOCHES

FelinesBat: LMA0

NATURELLLE: SMOOOOCHES TOO LOL

Cyran4life: THANX CUTIE <SMOOCHEROO>

FelinesBat: UH 0H
Cyran4life: **«·‾v^{•VIPER8995, is Off-Line•}^v‾·»**
Cyran4life: HEH
Cyran4life: BAHAHAHAHAHA
NATURELLLE: **<,Ordering sandwiches   ok whatcha all want?**
FelinesBat: LMCWSA0
Mikes36000: later all going for adip
Cyran4life: CRAZY WHITE STUPID?
Gusgus2: hi
Cyran4life: BYE MIKES
R0NI: **{{{{{{{{{{{{JAYJAY}}}}}}}}}}}}DYN 0 MIIIIIIITE**
NATURELLLE: **<<gonna have a fireball lol**
Cyran4life: **{{{{{{{{{{RICEAR0NI}}}}}}}}}}}}}}}}}}THE HELL YEAH I WANT SOME** TREAT
Cyran4life: LOL
Gusgus2: bye
FelinesBat: LMA0
Cyran4life: OK NOW WHO KNOWS HOW A PUNTER WORKS?
FelinesBat: U CLICK DE PUNT BUTTON, LMA0
NATURELLLE: <doesnt know CY   wanta teach me i need private lessons
R0NI: {S WHENAM~1
Cyran4life: NEXT WRONG ANSWER GETS MAH FOOT IN YO ASS
Cyran4life: LOL
Cyran4life: DAMN I CAN'T BELIEVE NOONE KNOWS
Mikes36000: cy you can come to bigggggggggg poolhell every body come
Cyran4life: COME ON PEOPLE
Rifle87608: HOW DOES A PUNTER WORK
Rifle87608: LOL
DPea625659: hello
Cyran4life: LOL
Cyran4life: RIFLE YOU KNOW?
EmraldEyez: CY.......LOL WHUTS the??
Mikes36000: pool party
OFL70: howdy room
FelinesBat: IT SENDZ A SHITLOAD OF MEMORY TO ANOTHER PUTER SO FAST DAT DA OTHER HARDDRIVE CANT TAKE AND
Cyran4life: HOW DOES A PUNTER WORK?
Rifle87608: «–•**CYRiX's** Punter Loaded by: Rifle87608•–»
FelinesBat: DEN BAMMMMMMMMM SEE YA

Rifle87608: **«–•CYRiX's Punter•–»** Anti-Pint Active
Cyran4life: CLOSE FELINE
Cyran4life: IT'S YOUR MODEM THAT CAN'T HANDLE MOST OF IT
FelinesBat: MY BAD
Cyran4life: THEN YOU LOSE YOUR SIGNAL
FelinesBat: JUST TELLIN IT HOW I WAS TOLD
EmraldEyez: LoL by sending tomuch info for your puter to acknowledge at 1 time..... ricieving an interne
Cyran4life: <PAT ON THE HEAD FOR FELINE>
NATURELLLE: <~~TAKING NOTES
FelinesBat: WAIT
Cyran4life: LMFAO
FelinesBat: IM A BAT !!
Spyfor007: <~~tenderedd
FelinesBat: LMCWSAO !!
Cyran4life: OH
Cyran4life: SORRY
Spyfor007: tenderess
Cali luver: **{{{{{{{{{{Family}}}}}}}}}}}}} {S jammy**
R0Nl: **{{{{{{{{{{{{{ROBYN}}}}}}}}}}}}}{S SLOBKISS**
FelinesBat: LMAO
NATURELLLE: **{{{{{{{{{{{{{{{{{{{{CALI}}}}}}}}}}}}}}}}}}** hi sweety
EmraldEyez: **{{{{{{{{{{{Robyn}}}}}}}}}}}]**
FelinesBat: **{{{{{{{{{{{{{{{{{R0BYN}}}}}}}}}}}}}}}}}**
Cyran4life: Laughing My Crazy White Stupid Ass Off?
NATURELLLE: <~~hates the feeling that ROBYN is now so far away
Cali luver: **{{{{{{{{{{RONI}}}}}}}}}}} {S slobkiss**
FelinesBat: NO
Cyran4life: what then?
EmraldEyez: LMFAOOOOO put that feline on the HEAD i dare ya hun
Rifle87608: MOST OF THER TIME IT EATS UP THE RAM
Cali luver: **{{{{{{{{{{NAT}}}}}}}}}}}**
FelinesBat: LAFFIN MY CAT WOMANZ SEXY AZZ OFF
FelinesBat: CAUSE SHE OWNZ ME
Cali luver: **{{{{{{{{{{{Barb}}}}}}}}}}}** love ya sis
Cyran4life: AAAAAAAAAAAAAAACCCCCCCCCCCCCCCCCKK KKKKKKKKKKKKKKKKKKKKKKKKKKKKKKKKKKKK KKKKKKKKKKKKKKKKK

Rifle87608:	CAUSES PAGE FAULT
Spyfor007:	gets out pet anaconda out of box
Cyran4life:	KATWOMN001?

Appendix Three

This Appendix is a listing of recordings I took from newsgroups at random. Not all postings to newsgroups contain pornographic pictures. Many times a lively debate can ensue or an encouragement can be issued to children to join the pornographic fun. Unfortunately, your children will not be having all that much fun if the pedophiles get their hands on them.

You may be shocked at the kinds of things said here. Keep in mind that newsgroups are generally anonymous. It is difficult to catch the sender and they are careful considering what they are doing. Review the examples below. It will provide ample motivation to any parent to monitor their children's activities online.

Example Number One

From - Mon Dec 22 19:13:24 1997
Path: news!global-news-master!newsfeed.concentric.net!199.0.154.56.MISMATCH!news2.ais.net!jamie!ais.net!howland.erols.net!news.alt.net!news.aa.net!news.aa.net!not-for-mail
From: Tosh <toshbliss@hotmail.com>
Newsgroups: alt.binaries.pictures.erotica.pre-teen
Subject: Re: ATTN!! I am 14 f & I need experienced help!!!
Date: Mon, 22 Dec 1997 14:54:07 -0700
Organization: Alternate Access Incorporated
Lines: 21
Message-ID: <35B65F7F.4DD7@hotmail.com>
References: <35b64b8a.3978382@news.chatcan.ca>
NNTP-Posting-Host: 206.98.108.73
Mime-Version: 1.0
Content-Type: text/plain; charset=us-ascii
Content-Transfer-Encoding: 7bit
X-Mailer: Mozilla 3.01 (Win95; I)
Xref: news alt.binaries.pictures.erotica.pre-teen:390792

Lucy September wrote:
>
> I am 14 years old and female babysitter
> I want to start experiementing with the kids I babysit but I have no idea what to do or where to
> start.
> I need someone who knows they are doing who I can keep coming back to for help and advice
> I need someone who doesnt think anything is gross and who will take this seriously
> I dont want jerks or idiots.
> Please. I am dead serious about this.
> Don't reply if you are going to be a jerk.
>
> Thanks

Okay, I'm gonna be a jerk...you have a serious stuttering problem, ya

know?
I have your message posted at least four times in a row...does this qualify as SPAM or what?

Tosh
The Gobblin' Girl
From the Mystery World

Example Number Two

From - Mon Dec 22 19:24:38 1997
Path: news!global-news-master!newsfeed.concentric.net!newsfeed.concentric.net!priori!news.he.net!Supernews60!supernews.com!Supernews69!not-for-mail
From: Herod@Jerusalem.com (Herod)
Newsgroups: alt.binaries.pictures.erotica.pre-teen
Subject: Re: POST TIME
Date: Mon, 22 Dec 1997 21:53:13 GMT
Organization: http://www.supernews.com, The World's Usenet: Discussions Start Here
Lines: 12
Message-ID: <35be5e54.28596596@news.supernews.com>
References: <35B63243.E84@school.net>
Reply-To: Herod@Jerusalem.net.
Mime-Version: 1.0
Content-Type: text/plain; charset=us-ascii
Content-Transfer-Encoding: 7bit
X-Trace: 901144360 GLHT7UMXH90ABD1D6 usenet36.supernews.com
X-Complaints-To: newsabuse@supernews.com
X-Newsreader: Forte Agent 1.5/32.452
Xref: news alt.binaries.pictures.erotica.pre-teen:390791

On Mon, 22 Dec 1997 11:41:07 -0700, NOODLES <noodles@school.net>
wrote:

>HOW'M I DOIN

Not too bad for a newbie, but you realize that a good bit of what you posted is really e-t rather than p-t. That's not a flame, simply an observation, first because you're trying, and second, because I believe you have no intent to spam the group. You do need to remember that unless it's part of a mixed series, that the group is pre-teen.

Herod

Example Number Three

From - Mon Aug 18 19:21:28 1997
Path: news!global-news-master!newsfeed.concentric.net!newsfeed.concentric.net!newshub.northeast.verio.net!europa.clark.net!208.134.241.18!newsfeed.internetmci.com!169.132.11.200!news.idt.net!novia!newscene.newscene.com!not-for-mail
From: god@tuna.can (Thunnus Thynnus)
Newsgroups: alt.binaries.pictures.erotica.pre-teen
Subject: Pedo U Faculty & Staff list (new release)
Date: 18 Aug 1997 17:32:06 -0500
Organization: Divine Tuna Can
Lines: 259
Message-ID: <MPG.1021d862704729a1989687@news1.newscene.com>
X-Newsreader: Anawave Gravity v2.00
Xref: news alt.binaries.pictures.erotica.pre-teen:390804

PEDO UNIVERSITY
LIST OF FACULTY AND STAFF
Official version 2.3, August 18, 1997

Questions or comments about this list should be posted to abpept, ATTN Schwuli von Prall.

Enrolment on the faculty and staff of Pedo U is by application. Applications should be directed to Dean Groucho.

To be eligible, an applicant should be a regular of the newsgroup (i.e. have participated for a period long enough to make him or her well known to the other regulars) and have posted on-topic pictures or text posts. Pictures need not be new, nor do they need to contain nudity. Pedo U does NOT demand or incite the posting of illegal material.

A note on assistants' names:
Names in double quotes are totally inofficial and usually bestowed by the Faculty and Staff members themselves. Names not in double quotes are official series names (or part of series names), or otherwise known to be the correct names of the girls in question.

HEAD OF PEDO U:

Groucho
Dean
Assistants: Laika, VEN08

GUARDIAN SAINT:

Dinkydow
Disciplinarian
Assistants: JOUJOU30

Dinks used to participate under a couple of other nicks as well:

Refried Dreams
Editor Emeritus of the Campus Yearbook
Assistants: Amysis

The Archbishop
Dean of Religious Studies
Assistants: Shelly

FACULTY AND STAFF:

Apostrophe
Dance Instructor
Assistants: All (under PU rules, limited to 2) of Disney's Mousercisers

Archangel
Special Liaison for Foreign Groups
Assistants: Anna Ancenis (LA_12), Michelle

Archivistt
Professor of Umbilicus Studies and Research
Assistants: Jenny, "Innie" (FEM-015)

Crusader Raider (aka Me)
Head of Debate Class; Editor-In-Chief of the Campus Newspaper
Assistants: "Katy" (CHSH), "Mindy Yowza" (J.L.M.32)

Cutter
Professor of Flat Plane Rhizomes
Assistants: POY46 (both girls)

Dr. Stein
Dean of Anatomical Studies and Pre-Admission Physicals
Assistants: "Dominique" (RO-12), Cindy

Fizzledick
Professor Emeritus, Lecturer in Pre-teen Pubic Development
Assistants: Tina (from the BYAKUYA series), Janet

Frank McCoy
Director, Family Counseling Office
Assistants:

Godfather
U.S. Customs Liaison
Assistants:

goober
Foreign Exchange Student Counselor
Assistants: Marian, Anna

Herod
Professor of Classical Studies
Assistants: "Misty Dawn" (JS-EG012)

HiNewbies
Doctor of Procrastination, Editor of the Campus Yearbook
Assistants: Tanya and Marina (MCLT7240's; BC_MT series)

JamieO
Associate Dean in Charge of the Faculty Coffee Pot
Assistants: "Creamy Dee" (D series), "Sugarbaby" (FW series)

Jerry Lee
Director of Music Department
Assistants:

Keenan
Music Instructor (Chorus, Jazz Band, Marching Band)
Assistants: Melodie, Sylvie (SYLYIE)

Kook A. Racha
Deputy, Pedo University Campus Police
Assistants: Danielle

Long Gone
Lieutenant, Pedo University Campus Police
Assistants: Sabrina, Valerie

Lurking Walter
Dean of Engineering
Assistants: "Cookie Brown" (ALS-0758)

Major Woody
Professor of Braille Anatomical Research
Assistants: Cathy (from the Yossy scans)

Max Thrott
Crash Studies Consultant; PU Gift Shoppe Director
Assistants: Olsen Twins, Lizzie Olsen

MMMelissa
Sex Education and Head Therapist
Assistants:

Pancho
Director of Dairy Applications; Equestrian Coach
Assistants: Miki

PeeWee
Chief of Pedo University Campus Police
Assistants: "Goldie" (GA-15), "Lydia" (LLD-034)

PiT
Director of Pubic Hygiene, W.B.G.
Assistants: Chiaki, Sophie (SP11 series)

PoppaCherry
Shower Room Monitor
Assistants: Eva (Ionesco), Jackdaw "socks" girl

Post' em

Library assistant (in the dark little room behind the last row of books);
Keeper of the LL-FAQ
Assistants: 43-01, Maria (A2-KI01 - 16)

Radar Rider
Director of the ETLF (Extra-Terrestrial Life Forms) Exploration Institute
Assistants: "Sandy" (LGLS1050), "Jane" (MCLT0199)

Rainman
Professor of Ecological Studies, Chief of the PU Campus Fire Station
Assistants: "Grace" (STATE-34), "Namie" (MCLT3218)

Robinson Crusoe
Vice-Chancellor of Drooling
Assistants: "Friday" (L011), "Munday" (50KDM)

Sarge
Security Director, C.L.I.T. (Center for Light Intensive Training)
Assistants: "Flo" (BC_FLO05), "Natalie" (CH_001)

Schwuli von Prall
Bulletproof Professor of Germanic Studies; Dean of Botany
Assistants: "Brünnhilde" (MCLT0152), "Columbine" (ALS-0879)

Spacedust
Campus Janitor
Assistants: HK, Shiori

Spiritwalker (aka Bungalow Bill, Lord of Canaria etc.)
Director, Early Childhood Education Department; Chairman, Nudeclear Physics
Department; Bartender, P.U. PUb
Assistants: Melissa (JPC-F018), Baudet31,37

The MadHatter
Professor of Literature; Offical Tea Party Coordinator
Assistants: Megumi (the chubby one), Kitty (aka Maria)

The New Afqizs
Pedo Educator to the Outside World; Pedo U Usenet Counsellor
Assistants: "Heather" (MT0061), Inga

Vesper

Spelling Tutor; Coach of Minor Sports & Cheerleading Squad
Assistants: Grandma Pink Slippers, Kattie (PLAY series)

Viper
Dean of English Department; Assistant Spelling Tutor
Assistants: AOI-079, Sascia

W.E. Goodrich
Director of Psychology
Assistants:

Whisper
Night Watchman
Assistants: Karen Christy (MCLT0459 - 0469), Maia (A2-MAIA)

wildman
Professor of Genealogy
Assistants: Julie

Witt
Dean of Philosophy
Assistants: Sophie, Vanessa

STAFF CHANGES
==============

NEW
Major Woody

RESIGNED
LTL, Tattooed

ON LEAVE
PM

IN MEMORIAM
============

Our dear friend Dinkydow has left this world. We shall miss him a lot, but let's hope there is an afterlife and that he is happily cuddling some little assistant in Pedo Heaven.

I have taken the liberty of making Dinks the Guardian Saint of Pedo U. Maybe he wasn't always a saint in this life, but he sure was a good friend. I hope nobody is offended by his elevation to saintly status; if you are, please let me know and suggest how else we can keep Dinks on our Faculty and Staff list.

S v P

Example Number Four

From - Mon Aug 18 19:37:21 1997
Path: news!global-news-master!newsfeed.concentric.net!199.0.154.56.MISMATCH!news2.ais.net!jamie!ais.net!newsfeed1.earthlink.net!newsfeed.concentric.net!web.net!not-for-mail
From: badboyme@webtv.net (badboy)
Newsgroups: alt.binaries.pictures.erotica.pre-teen
Subject: Re: POST TIME
Date: Mon, 18 Aug 1997 12:25:25 -0400 (EDT)
Organization: Web Subscriber
Lines: 2
Message-ID: <15655-35B61275-26@newsd-111.bryant.web.net>
References: <35B630CA.4A9B@school.net>
NNTP-Posting-Host: localhost.web.net
Mime-Version: 1.0 (Web)
Content-Type: Text/Plain; Charset=US-ASCII
Content-Transfer-Encoding: 7Bit
X-WebTV-Signature: 1
ETAuAhUAgsbvYulVhDqKothmtXAEuCY1fvsCFQDCZmsBRIUgTfRulijgmE4Cuh7F6A==
Xref: news alt.binaries.pictures.erotica.pre-teen:390611

Great mpeg. Have any younger ones? Please post. Thanks

Example Number Five

From - Mon Aug 18 19:38:39 1997
Path: news!global-news-master!newsfeed.concentric.net!199.0.154.56.MISMATCH!news2.ais.net!jamie!ais.net!cpk-news-hub1.bbnplanet.com!news.bbnplanet.com!Supernews60!supernews.com!Supernews69!not-for-mail
From: Post@them.now (Post 'em)
Newsgroups: alt.binaries.pictures.erotica.pre-teen
Subject: Post 'em / ping---DOM, Fizz
Date: Fri, 15 Aug 1997 00:03:34 GMT
Organization: http://www.supernews.com, The World's Usenet: Discussions Start Here
Lines: 6
Message-ID: <35b67d19.930175@news.infopool.com>
Reply-To: Post@them.now
Mime-Version: 1.0
Content-Type: text/plain; charset=us-ascii
Content-Transfer-Encoding: 7bit
X-Trace: 901152836 VZXIPFER1BFADD0FE usenet42.supernews.com
X-Complaints-To: newsabuse@supernews.com
X-Newsreader: Forte Agent 1.01/32.397
Xref: news alt.binaries.pictures.erotica.pre-teen:390869

I just got back from my mini-vaction.
I had a HARD time lookiong at those 10 - 14 year olds in their swimsuits. Whis I could have brought back some pics for everyone to enjoy.
LL-series--->fire when ready.
Post 'em

Example Number Six

From - Wed Sep 17 19:42:09 1997
Path: news!global-news-master!newsfeed.concentric.net!newsfeed.concentric.net!newsfeed.direct.ca!Supernews73!supernews.com!Supernews69!not-for-mail
From: DOM <lurker@thresh.old>
Newsgroups: alt.binaries.pictures.erotica.pre-teen
Subject: Re: In rememberance. A little peek - candid1.jpg(1/1)
Date: Wed, 17 Sep 1997 14:18:06 -0500
Organization: http://www.supernews.com, The World's Usenet: Discussions Start Here
Lines: 11
Message-ID: <35B63ACC.32BA@thresh.old>
References: <6p2g8frsf1@usenet51.supernews.com> <35b3cd7b.79488665@news.mindspring.com>
NNTP-Posting-Host: 208.134.149.115
Mime-Version: 1.0
Content-Type: text/plain; charset=us-ascii
Content-Transfer-Encoding: 7bit
X-Trace: 901135037 XDE.3SBPW9573D086C usenet88.supernews.com
X-Complaints-To: newsabuse@supernews.com
X-Mailer: Mozilla 3.01-C-MACOS8 (Macintosh; I; PPC)
Xref: news alt.binaries.pictures.erotica.pre-teen:390729

Nobody wrote:
>
> wrote:
>
>>
>>[Saved as file: C:\WINDOWS\DESKTOP\candid1.jpg]
> Cool !! Somebody reposts my posts! Hope y'all like 'em!

How'd you do these, thru the peep in your front door?

DOM

Example Number Seven

From - Wed Sep 17 19:43:32 1997
Path: news!global-news-master!newsfeed.concentric.net!199.0.154.56.MISMATCH!news2.ais.net!jamie!ais.net!europa.clark.net!4.1.16.34!cpk-news-hub1.bbnplanet.com!news.bbnplanet.com!wn3feed!135.173.83.25!wn4feed!worldnet.att.net!207.14.113.10!news.alt.net!usenet
From: just@little.lover© (wildman©)
Newsgroups: alt.binaries.pictures.erotica.pre-teen
Subject: Re: Hmmm.
Date: 17 Sep 1997 20:22:14 GMT
Organization: nowhere.fast
Lines: 31
Message-ID: <6p5hlm$8p1$1@dosa.alt.net>
References: <01bdb553$6db91100$4cbc9ace@williefe>
Reply-To: anywhere@you.like
X-Newsreader: WinVN 0.99.8 (x86 32bit)
Xref: news alt.binaries.pictures.erotica.pre-teen:390754

In article <01bdb553$6db91100$4cbc9ace@williefe>, me , me@me tossed this
thought out into the electronic ether for all of us here to read, and said.......
>
>
> You guys are pretty sick. Seriously - tell me the pleasure you get out of
>these pics? I'm really being serious and want real answers - not just
>flames. Aren't you guys afraid you're going to get caught? Doesn't your
>servers monitor this stuff?
>
I gather you are serious; after all you said it twice.
Now for the matter at hand, where am I posting from? See, you don't have a
clue. There's no ISP listed in my headers. So how would you or anyone be able
to find me to have me arrested?
And as far as the server I am using, he will not look at the content of this

NG; if he did he would probably be accused of some sort of crime. The server is
merely a common carrier, and as such is not responsible for monitoring the
content of any NG, else he would be guilty of complicity were there any wrongdoing.
Now why don't you find yourself some NG somewhere where they are talking about
putting together nuclear devices. You might actually be doing mankind a favor
if you could shut down that sort of NG.
And be sure not to let that slimy rock squash you when you slither back under
it. Thank you, and have a nice day!!!
--
ILWT
wildman
Professor of Genealogy
Pedo University

Example Number Eight

From - Wed Sep 17 19:44:41 1997
Path: news!global-news-master!newsfeed.concentric.net!199.0.154.56.MISMATCH!news2.ais.net!jamie!ais.net!howland.erols.net!worldfeed.gte.net!nntp.giganews.com!news.giganews.com.POSTED!not-for-mail
Newsgroups: alt.binaries.pictures.erotica.pre-teen
From: Pekpojida@mindspring.com (Sir Rantsalot¤)
Subject: Re: Hmmm.
Organization: FreeMe
References: <01bdb553$6db91100$4cbc9ace@williefe>
X-Newsreader: News Xpress 2.01
Lines: 27
Message-ID: <7uqt1.1585$K4.1787829@news.giganews.com>
Date: Wed, 17 Sep 1997 18:48:35 GMT
NNTP-Posting-Host: 209.99.40.7
NNTP-Posting-Date: Wed, 17 Sep 1997 13:48:35 CDT
Xref: news alt.binaries.pictures.erotica.pre-teen:390688

In article <01bdb553$6db91100$4cbc9ace@williefe>, "me" <me@me> wrote:
>
> You guys are pretty sick. Seriously - tell me the pleasure you get out of
>these pics? I'm really being serious and want real answers - not just
>flames. Aren't you guys afraid you're going to get caught? Doesn't your
>servers monitor this stuff?
>

No. We are all hackers and members of the internet and computer industry, usually high up. We control who gets what, and the ISP's know this. Without us, they would crash in a day. Piss us off, and we could bring down all their systems.

That's why they leave us alone, and that's why you don't see many really stupid thumpers and really nasty people last too long here; they just somehow "disappear" from here.

You see, most members of the intelligentsia of the computer industry, are pedophiles.

The FBI and congress knows this, and that's why we are here, free, and unafraid. We actually rule the world, in a back-door sort of way.

There are two people you don't want to really piss off in this world: People who run your computers, and Alan Greenspan.

Understand?

Go ahead and dl some pics, take a look around. You know you want to. Trust me, you're safe here with us.
Welcome to complete freedom like you've never seen before.

N.P.L.F.

Example Number Nine

From - Wed Sep 17 19:55:38 1997
Path: news!global-news-master!newsfeed.concentric.net!nntp-out.monmouth.com!newspeer.monmouth.com!newsfeed.internetmci.com!204.156.128.20!news1.best.com!nntp2.ba.best.com!not-for-mail
From: hello@spam.com (Black & White Books)
Newsgroups: alt.binaries.pictures.erotica.early-teens
Subject: ~very pretty www.nudebooks.com - afate44.jpg [1/1]
Date: 17 Sep 1997 21:56:56 GMT
Organization: Black & White Books
Lines: 762
Message-ID: <6p5n78$ee1$4@nntp2.ba.best.com>
NNTP-Posting-Host: dynamic51.pm11.sf3d.best.com
X-Trace: 901144616 14785 (none) 206.86.0.12
X-Newsreader: WinVN 0.99.8 (x86 32bit)
Xref: news alt.binaries.pictures.erotica.early-teens:203813

--
Item: RON OLIVER
Photographer: AS FAR AS THE EYE CAN SEE
**** FIND OUT MORE! ****
This item is described and available for sale at my website.
Look in the "OTHER NUDES (M-Z)" section of the Table of Contents
The address is: www.nudebooks.com
There are 150 Nude Photography Books/Magazines/Videos -
out of print, hard-to-find, and many imports, with a picture from
each item.
** OVER 21 ONLY ** ** ALL BOOKS ARE LEGAL **
BLACK & WHITE BOOKS
41 SUTTER, SUITE 1056
SAN FRANCISCO, CA 94104-4987 USA
(415) 931-3349
mail-order only
VISA ** MC ** AMEX ** MONEY ORDER
www.nudebooks.com
Occasionally the server goes down due to technical difficulties.
If it's down, try visiting again at the top of the hour. Thanks.
(All books sold by Black & White Books have been reviewed by an

attorney and are legal. We do not sell "child pornography" as that term is defined under applicable laws, nor do we have any intent to violate such laws. Our books are intended to describe and portray the human body and condition in all its aspects. We invite all people, regardless of sexual persuasion, to visit our site. However, we do not pander to anyone's prurient sexual interests.)

Example Number Ten

From - Wed Sep 17 20:51:54 1997
Path: news!global-news-master!newsfeed.concentric.net!199.0.154.56.MISMATCH!news2.ais.net!jamie!ais.net!news-peer.gip.net!news.gsl.net!gip.net!portc01.blue.aol.com!audrey03.news.aol.com!not-for-mail
From: kinkou69@aol.com (KinkoU69)
Newsgroups: alt.binaries.pictures.erotica.bestiality
Subject: K9 girls are you out there
Lines: 1
Message-ID: <1998072222025100.SAA18429@ladder03.news.aol.com>
NNTP-Posting-Host: ladder03.news.aol.com
X-Admin: news@aol.com
Date: 17 Sep 1997 22:02:50 GMT
Organization: AOL http://www.aol.com
Xref: news alt.binaries.pictures.erotica.bestiality:274454

I need to see you and dog get it on in PA,MD,DE,NJ will pay to watch

Supple Publishing offers quantity discounts to corporations, non-profit organizations, libraries, bookstores and individuals.

If you require additional copies of this book contact Supple Publishing at:

1535 Plank Road
Menasha, WI 54952

You can also contact us by phone at:

920-725-5331

Or on the Internet at:

KeithTaxFr@aol.com

If you would like the author, Keith Schroeder, to speak to your group or organization, contact Supple Publishing for available times.

Supple Publishing and Keith Schroeder thank you for purchasing this book. Comments are welcome.

Keith Schroeder was born in Chilton, Wisconsin in 1964. He began writing in the early 1980's and began publishing technical material in 1989. Mr. Schroeder is a General Partner in a real estate investment company and the owner of a tax and accounting firm. He has helped numerous businesses set up and protect their computer systems. Mr. Schroeder now enjoys quiet evenings on his hobby farm near Hilbert, Wisconsin with his wife Sue, his daughter, Heather, and two very friendly kitty cats. He is currently working on his next book.